29-0

World Tourism Organization

ties on TOURISM

30

A TOURISM AND ENVIRONMENT PUBLICATION

foreword

Ensuring the sustainability of tourism has become the main challenge of those involved in the development and management of this vibrant sector of activity, which is bound to grow over the next decades at at least similar rates as it has during the last quarter of this century.

The continued growth of this industry and its associated tendency to overcrowding, progresses in line with a stronger environmental awareness of consumers who will increasingly demand cleaner, safer and more environment-friendly tourist destinations. These two trends, one quantitative and the other qualitative, make it imperative to develop and manage a sustainable tourism industry.

Although the tourism sector of a country is for the most part developed, funded and managed by private companies and individuals, the responsibilities of the public sector in securing its long-term sustainability are as important as those of private operators.

This is because, first, a substantial proportion of the tourism services consumed by tourists is normally supplied by national, regional or local public institutions, although more often than not, these services do not have a market price. Second, the central and/or local authorities set the rules of the game in a number of areas that impinge on the form in which tourism develops in a particular country or locality. Therefore, for tourism to develop in an economically and environmentally sustainable manner, adequate coordination of such rules and regulations needs to be guaranteed. And third, it remains the responsibility of the public sector to oversee the observance of the agreed rules and regulations by all the players involved in the development and management of tourism.

With this book, the World Tourism Organization intends to strengthen its efforts to achieve tourism sustainability worldwide. It particularly seeks to provide technical guidelines and methodological instruments to local authorities, public service officials operating at the local level, as well as private tourism developers, enabling them to assume their responsibilities in this field with more effective, up-to-date technical know-how. These guidelines are eminently practical and easy to apply. The numerous examples of sustainable tourism best practices contained in this volume and the supplementary volumes on sub-Saharan Africa, Asia and the Pacific, North Africa and the Americas should be readily adaptable to the particular conditions and level of development of each country, region and local territory.

WTO urges all central, regional and local governments and tourism companies in general, to follow the principles and guidelines contained in this book to ensure that tourism in their territories is sustainable in the long term.

Francesco Frangialli
Secretary-General
World Tourism Organization

acknowledgements

This guide is a new and entirely revised version of WTO's *Sustainable Tourism Development: Guide for Local Planners* published in 1993. It was prepared and written by Edward Inskeep, a WTO consultant in tourism planning, research and training.

Edward Inskeep is a tourism development planner who has been a WTO consultant for about 20 years, leading teams of experts in a good number of technical co-operation projects executed by WTO in many countries, especially in Africa, Asia and the Pacific.

Mr. Inskeep has used the experience he has accumulated from his active involvement in these projects in the preparation of this guide.

WTO's Chief of Environment and Planning, Eugenio Yunis, has been instrumental in the review and editing of this guide and has benefited from the assistance of Christine Brew.

Cover design and layout: Eril Wiehahn
Production Coordinator: Diane Palumbo
Printed by: Egraf S.A., Madrid

contents

ANNEXES 163

BIBLIOGRAPHY 191

FIGURES

PURPOSE OF THIS GUIDE

Local authorities responsible for counties, districts, cities, towns, villages, rural areas and attraction sites are increasingly becoming more involved in developing and managing many aspects of tourism. This is in line with the trend in many countries toward decentralisation of government to give more responsibility to local authorities. These authorities often know better what is in their own best interest and will strive to achieve local development objectives.

introduction

It also reflects the emphasis now being given to community involvement in tourism, with local communities participating in the tourism planning and development process of their areas. Through participation, the communities receive greater benefits from tourism in the form of employment and income, opportunities for establishing tourism enterprises and other advantages. By receiving benefits from tourism, the communities will give greater support to this sector.

Many local authorities, however, do not yet have much experience in planning, developing and managing tourism. Consequently, their efforts in tourism may be misdirected, thereby wasting valuable resources. Proper planning, efficient implementation of development and effective continuous management of tourism are essential if the benefits of tourism to local areas are to be optimised, and any potential problems minimised. To assist local authorities in making better decisions on developing tourism, this guide has been prepared on the planning, development and management of tourism at the local level. The guide will also be very useful to regional and national tourism agencies who need to understand tourism development at the local level in order to provide direction and assistance to local authorities.

An underlying principle of this guide is achieving sustainable development of tourism. The fundamental importance of the sustainable approach for all types of development including tourism is now universally accepted, if not always practised as it should be. Sustainability is based on global policies set forth in the landmark study, Our Common Future, the 1987 report prepared by the World Commission on Environment and Development to the United Nations General Assembly. This report defined a sustainable society as one that "meets the needs of the present without compromising the ability of future generations to meet their own needs." At the United Nations Conference on Environment and Development, popularly known as the Earth Summit and held in Rio de Janeiro in 1992, the sustainable development approach was further elaborated and expressed in Agenda 21 which was adopted by the conference, followed by the Agenda 21 for the Travel and Tourism Industry, issued later by the **World Tourism Organization** and other organisations in 1995. Many national governments have now adopted sustainability as their fundamental development policy.

This guide is a revision and updating of the popular Sustainable Tourism Development: Guide for Local Planners, published by the **World Tourism Organization** in 1993. The guide presents concepts, principles and techniques for planning, developing and managing tourism at the local level. It is essential that the tourism sector be integrated with other local sectors and with national and regional tourism development policies and plans. Therefore, the guide also examines how to achieve integration of the local tourism sector.

This guide is a general one designed for use in many types of local situations. Each area, however, has its own particular environmental, cultural and institutional characteristics and approaches to development, and tourism planning, development and management must be adapted to each local situation. The regional guides to be prepared in this series will provide more specific guidance on developing tourism at the local level for each of the world's major geographic and cultural regions — Asia and the Pacific, Sub-Saharan Africa, the Middle East and North Africa and the Americas; they will appear during 1998 and 1999.

HOW TO USE THIS GUIDE

The guide is structured around seven major sections:

SECTION 1

Tourism in Today's World provides the essential background. It presents an overview of the importance of tourism globally, tourism trends that local authorities should be aware of, concepts of sustainable tourism and the levels of tourism planning and development.

SECTION 2

Tourism in Your Community shows the relationship of tourism to local communities. It reviews the benefits and problems of tourism, the tourism system, the relationship of tourism to the environment and community, and how to evaluate resources for developing tourism.

SECTION 3

Planning for Local Tourism Development presents tourism planning concepts, processes and standards. It focuses on tourism planning approaches, the tourism planning process including carrying capacity analysis, process of developing tourism projects, environmental impact assessment, and tourist facility development, design and quality standards.

SECTION 4

Planning Principles for Tourism Development sets forth basic principles to be applied in preparing development plans for tourism in sub-regions and local areas, resorts, urban tourism, ecotourism, the many other forms of tourism, and for various types of tourist attractions and activities. Careful management of visitor use of tourist attractions is stressed.

SECTION 5

Implementing Tourism Development examines how to implement tourism plans and achieve development objectives. It reviews the respective roles of the public and private sectors, sets forth implementation approaches and techniques and explores the important considerations of project programming, financing tourism, human resource development for tourism, how to involve local communities, and approaches to marketing and promotion of tourism.

SECTION 6

Maintaining the Sustainability of Tourism looks specifically at achieving sustainability of this sector. It examines the three major aspects of achieving sustainable tourism development: managing the environmental impacts of tourism, managing socio-economic impacts and maintaining the tourism product and tourist markets. The concept of establishing and applying environmental indicators to measure sustainability is explained.

SECTION 7

Managing the Tourism Sector reviews the approaches to achieve effective management of tourism at the local level. It emphasises the importance of management, and describes management functions and organisation for management. Several important management functions are examined: establishing a tourism information system, monitoring tourism development, carrying out public tourism awareness programmes and informing tourists, tourist safety and security, maintaining the vitality of the tourism sector, coping with saturation and crisis management.

The guide also includes several annexes which set forth important statements on aspects of tourism that will be useful to local authorities. Annex 1 is the Tourism Bill of Rights which is basic to the development of the tourism sector in any area. Other annexes relate to specific topics that are referred to in the guide.

This is an interactive guide that involves its users. It includes checklists, diagrams and questions for discussion by local authorities about developing tourism in their areas.

AN OVERVIEW

Tourism has become one of the major socio-economic sectors in the world and one of the leading components of international trade. In 1997, there were 612 million international tourist arrivals who generated US$443 billion in foreign exchange receipts. By the year 2020, the World Tourism Organization **(WTO) projects that there will be about 1.6 billion international tourist arrivals and international tourism receipts will reach $2 trillion. Domestic**

SECTION

tourism in today's world

1

tourism is estimated to be about ten times that of international tourism globally. Both international and domestic tourism are expanding rapidly in developing countries as they develop their tourism sectors and become more prosperous. Tourism includes both holiday and business travellers as well as persons travelling for other purposes. Planning must be carried out for all these types of tourists, all of whom require facilities and services and spend money in the local area.

There are several influencing trends in tourism that local authorities should be aware of in their planning of tourism. A basic trend is that more tourists wish to participate in recreation, sports and adventure and learn about the history, culture and natural environment of areas they visit. Special interest and adventure tourism are expanding rapidly as are other specialised forms of tourism including cultural, nature, 'roots', health and religious tourism. Ecotourism has become very popular. Many tourists are seeking new destinations and new types of tourism products. More tourists are environmentally sensitive and wish to visit destinations that are well planned and do not create environmental or social problems. Business travel and travel to attend conferences and meetings will continue expanding.

The concept of sustainable development including sustainable tourism development has been adopted by the United Nations, the WTO and many national, regional and local governments. Sustainable tourism implies that the natural, historic and cultural resources for tourism are conserved for continuous use in the future as well as the present. In fact,

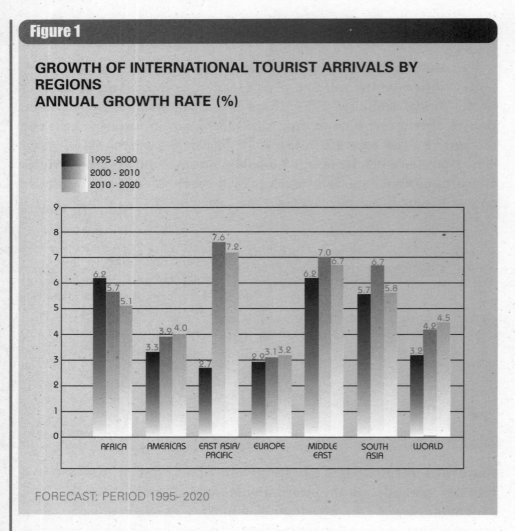

Figure 1

GROWTH OF INTERNATIONAL TOURIST ARRIVALS BY REGIONS
ANNUAL GROWTH RATE (%)

1995 -2000
2000 - 2010
2010 - 2020

FORECAST: PERIOD 1995- 2020

these resources can be enhanced by tourism where needed. Sustainable tourism also means that tourism development does not generate serious environmental or sociocultural problems, the overall environmental quality of the tourism area is maintained or improved, a high level of tourist satisfaction is maintained so that tourist markets are retained and the benefits of tourism are widely spread throughout the society. Agenda 21 is a comprehensive programme of action adopted at the Earth Summit in 1992. Within this framework, the WTO and other agencies have prepared an Agenda 21 for the Travel and Tourism Industry which sets forth the role that travel and tourism must perform in achieving sustainable development.

Tourism planning is carried out at various levels from the international, national and regional to the local or community level. Tourism planning and development must be integrated among all these levels. This guide focuses on the local level, but local authorities must take into account regional and national tourism policies and plans, so that the respective levels reinforce one another to make a stronger tourism sector.

THE IMPORTANCE OF TOURISM

Tourism has emerged as one of the world's major socio-economic sectors, and has been steadily expanding at an average rate of about 4-5 per cent annually during the latter half of the 20th century. The combination of domestic and international tourism is now acknowledged as comprising the world's 'largest industry'. In 1995, tourism globally generated an estimated US$3.4 trillion in gross output, contributing 10.9 per cent of the world's gross domestic product (GDP), creating employment for about 212 million people and producing US$637 billion in government tax revenues.

International tourism is one of the leading components of international trade. In 1997, there were 612 million international tourist arrivals. The term 'tourist arrivals' refers to total international tourist

Figure 2

INTERNATIONAL TOURIST ARRIVALS BY REGIONS

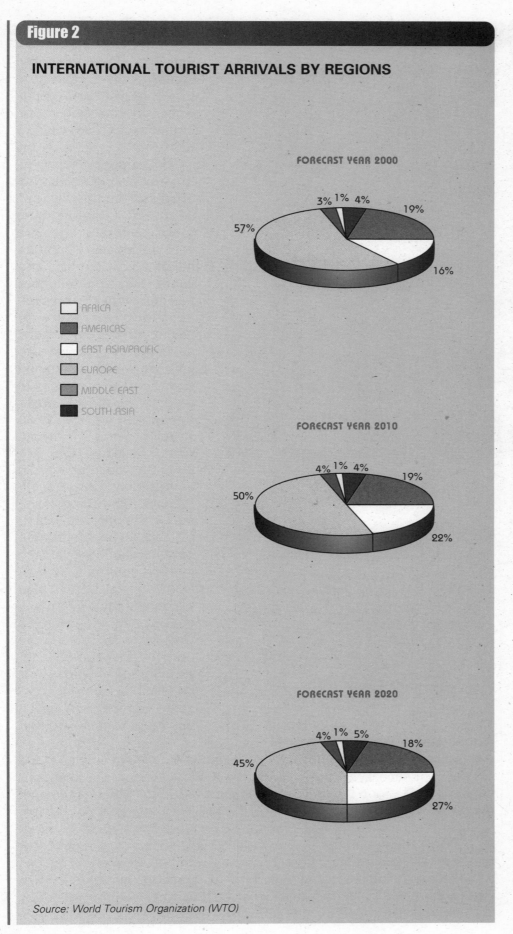

Source: World Tourism Organization (WTO)

trips made, not to the number of different tourists travelling. Some persons take more than one international trip per year. These tourist arrivals generated a total of US$443 billion in foreign exchange. This figure does not include the large amount of money spent on air fares and other means of international travel. The majority of international tourists are short and medium-haul, that is they travel within their own global region. Long-haul travel among different regions is, however, very important for many places.

Although specific figures are not available on a global basis, domestic tourism is estimated to be about ten times that of international tourism based on tourist trips taken. Domestic tourism receipts (expenditures by tourists in the local area) are considerably greater in total than international tourism receipts.

Tourism is already an important activity in many big/large countries, contributing up to 5-10 percent of national GDP. In some small countries, and especially for several small island nations in the Caribbean, Mediterranean, Pacific and Indian Ocean areas, tourism represents 20-25 per cent of the GDP. In many places where tourism is still a minor sector, it is expanding rapidly and will become more important in the future. However, as demonstrated

Figure 3

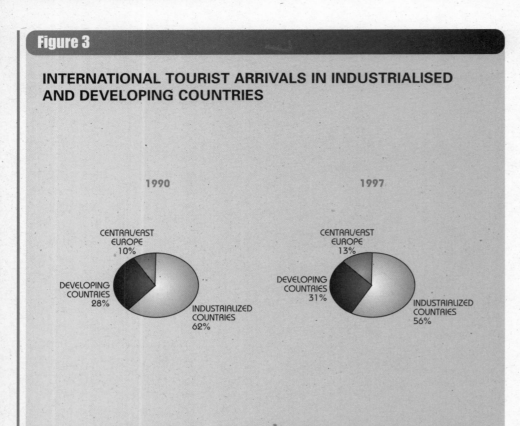

INTERNATIONAL TOURIST ARRIVALS IN INDUSTRIALISED AND DEVELOPING COUNTRIES

COUNTRY GROUPINGS	TOURIST ARRIVALS (000)			% CHANGE		MARKET SHARE	% OF WORLD TOTAL
	1990	1996	1997	97/96	97/90	1990	1997
World Total	457,647	594,827	612,835	3.03	4.26	100,00	100,00
Industrialized countries	283,823	331,473	347,075	4.71	2.92	62.02	56.63
Developing Countries	130,015	182,578	187,390	2.64	5.36	28.41	30.58
Central/East Europe	43,809	80,776	78,370	-2.98	8.66	9.57	12.79

Source: World Tourism Organization (WTO)

in **Figure 2**, most of the global regions, as well as many countries and many areas within countries, have not yet even come close to realising their potential in developing tourism.

The industrialised or more developed countries received about 56 per cent of international tourist arrivals in 1996 with developing countries including Central and Eastern Europe receiving the remainder. However, as shown in **Figure 3**, based on current trends, developing countries are receiving an increasing share of international tourists as they improve transportation access, develop tourist attractions, facilities and services and become known as desirable tourist destinations. The East Asia-Pacific Region, for example, has been the fastest growing region over the past several years. Domestic tourism is also expanding rapidly in many developing countries as they become more prosperous, resulting in expanding middle class populations with disposable incomes, and develop appropriate tourist attractions, facilities and services.

International tourism is projected to continue growing at about 4.0 and 4.5 per cent annually as shown in **Figure 1.** WTO projects that there will be about 659 million international tourist arrivals in the year 2000, about one billion in 2010 and approximately 1.6 billion arrivals in 2020. Tourism receipts (total expenditures of international tourists) will reach $2 trillion by 2020. By then, one out of every four arrivals will be long-haul, that is tourists travelling among different world regions. All the world's regions will experience substantial growth in international tourism as shown in **Figure 2.** Domestic tourism is also expected to continue growing rapidly in all the regions.

DEFINITION OF TOURISM AND TOURISTS

It is important to understand what is meant by tourism and tourists. The **World Tourism Organization** has developed a series of "Recommendations on Tourism Statistics" issued from the 1991 Ottawa Conference and which were officially adopted by the United Nations Statistical Commission in 1993. The important aspects of these definitions can be summarised as follows:

Definition of tourism

- **Tourism:** The activities of persons travelling to and staying in places outside of their usual environment for not more than one consecutive year for leisure, business and other purposes.
- **Domestic tourism:** Involves residents of the given country travelling only within the country.
- **Inbound tourism:** Involves non-residents travelling in the given country.
- **Outbound tourism:** Involves residents travelling in another country.
- **International tourism:** Consists of inbound and outbound tourism.
- **Tourism expenditure:** The total consumption expenditure made by a visitor or on behalf of a visitor for and during his/her trip and stay at the destination.

Definition of tourist

- **International visitor:** Any person who travels to a country other than that in which he/she has his/her usual residence and outside his/her usual environment for a period not exceeding 12 months and whose main purpose of visit is other than the exercise of an activity remunerated from within the country visited.

- **Domestic visitor:** Any person residing in a country who travels to a place within the country and outside his/her usual environment for a period not exceeding 12 months and whose main purpose of visit is other than the exercise of an activity remunerated from within the place visited.

- **Overnight visitor:** Any visitor who stays at least one night in collective or private accommodation in the place visited.

- **Same-day visitor:** Any visitor who does not spend the night in collective or private accommodation in the place visited. This definition includes cruise passengers who arrive in a country on a cruise ship and return to the ship each night to sleep on board even though the ship remains in port for several days. Also included in this group are, by extension, owners or passengers of yachts and passengers on a group tour accommodated in a train.

These definitions are elaborated and other classifications and definitions are indicated in **Figure 4** which sets forth the official definitions.

It is important that international tourists be classified by place of usual residence as well as nationality. Many people live in countries different than their country of nationality. For marketing and other purposes, the

Figure 4

DEFINITION OF TOURISM AND TOURIST

TOURISM
Comprises the activities of persons travelling to and staying in places outside their usual environment for not more than one consecutive year for leisure, business and other purposes.

INTERNATIONAL VISITOR
For statistical purposes, the term "international visitor" describes "any person who travels to a country other than that in which s/he has his/her usual residence but outside his/her usual environment for a period not exceeding 12 months, and whose main purpose of visit is other than the exercise of an activity remunerated from within the country visited"

TOURIST (overnight visitors)
A visitor who stays at least one night in a collective or private accommodation in the country or place visited.

SAME-DAY VISITOR
A visitor who does not spend the night in a collective or private accommodation in the country or place visited. This definition includes cruise passengers who arrive in a country on a cruise ship and return to the ship each night to sleep on board even though the ship remains in port for several days. Also included in this group are, by extension owners or passengers of yachts and passengers on a group tour accommodated in a train.

DOMESTIC VISITOR
For statistical purposes, the term "domestic visitor" describes any person residing in a country, who travels to a place within the country, outside his/her usual environment for a period not exceeding 12 months, and whose main purpose of visit is other than the exercise of an activity remunerated from within the place visited."

DOMESTIC TOURISM
Involves residents of a given country travelling only within this country.

INBOUND TOURISM
Involves non-residents travelling in a given country.

OUTBOUND TOURISM
Involves residents travelling in another country.

INTERNAL TOURISM
Comprises domestic and inbound tourism.

NATIONAL TOURISM
Comprises domestic tourism and outbound tourism.

INTERNATIONAL TOURISM
Consists of inbound tourism and outbound tourism.

SOURCE : "Recommendations on Tourism Statistics" World Tourism Organization

place of residence of tourists is more important than their nationality.

Local authorities should note that tourists include persons travelling for business purposes and to attend meetings and conferences, and these types of tourists must be included in planning for tourism development. In fact, many areas encourage development of meeting and conference tourism to attract more tourists. Business tourists require many of the same facilities and services as do holiday tourists and spend money in the local area. Also many business travellers will spend part of their time being holiday tourists, making local tours and visiting attractions sites if these are available, thus increasing their expenditures in the local area.

Tourism is now viewed as an integrated socio-economic sector. For purposes of calculating the economic contribution of tourism in national and regional accounts, the WTO and other agencies have proposed, through the United Nations Statistical Commission, a change in national accounting procedures to include an item for the tourism sector and that all tourism expenditures be incorporated under this item. This accounting procedure will make it easier to separate out the contribution of the tourism sector and recognise its economic importance, in terms of contribution to Gross Domestic Product, in national accounts.

MAJOR TOURISM TRENDS

Local authorities must understand major tourism trends internationally in order to plan for tourism development that meets present and future expectations of tourists and accomplishes sustainability of the tourism sector. In addition to international trends, the local authorities should determine their own national, regional and local trends as a basis for planning for domestic tourism. In many places, international and domestic tourism trends will be similar.

Quantitative growth trends were examined in the previous section on the importance of tourism. Significant qualitative trends include the following:

- More tourists are desiring to participate in recreation, sports and adventure and learn about the history, culture, nature and wildlife of areas they visit. Tourists are more physically and intellectually active now than previously.

- More tourists wish to pursue their special interests and hobbies. There are many types of special interest tourism based on nature and wildlife, historic sites, cultural patterns, economic activities and professional interests.

- 'Roots' tourism of tourists visiting their ancestral home areas is becoming important in many places. Nature, cultural and adventure tourism are rapidly growing forms of tourism development. Religious tourism of persons visiting sacred sites related to their religious beliefs will remain a significant type of tourism.

- More tourists are seeking new destinations and new tourism products. This provides many opportunities to develop new tourism areas and improve and expand existing destinations.

- More tourists are concerned about maintaining and improving their health and there is much development of health resorts and spas. Conventional hotels and resorts are including exercise facilities. There is renewed interest in traditional medical treatments and these can form the basis for health resorts and special interest tourism.

- Many tourists are taking more frequent but shorter vacation throughout the year. This provides the opportunity to develop more tourist destinations, and for destinations to offer facilities and activities for tourists to use during different seasons throughout the year.

II Sustainable tourism development meets the needs of present tourists and host regions while protecting and enhancing opportunities for the future. It is envisaged as leading to management of all resources in such a way that economic, social, and aesthetic needs can be fulfilled while maintaining cultural integrity, essential ecological processes, biological diversity, and life support systems. II

- More older and active retired persons, many of who are affluent, are travelling. However, younger and middle aged people are still travelling in large numbers. More handicapped persons are travelling as tourists and facilities and services are being designed to handle handicapped tourists.

- Tourists are becoming more experienced and sophisticated in their travel habits and expect good quality attractions, facilities and services, and 'good value for money' in their travel expenditures.

- Business travel and conference/ meeting tourism will continue expanding and can bring benefits to many places. Many persons travelling on business or to attend conferences and meetings also function as holiday tourists during part of their stay in an area.

- More tourists are becoming environmentally and socially sensitive and seek well designed, less polluted tourist destinations, bypassing badly planned destinations that have environmental and social problems.

- More tourist destinations are adopting the planned and managed approach to developing tourism and wish to develop good quality tourism that avoids environmental and social problems and optimises economic benefits.

- Older tourist resorts are being upgraded and revitalised to meet present-day tourists' expectations, with this renovation being carried out in a carefully planned manner.

- The tourism sector is making increasing use of modern technology, in areas such as reservation services and marketing. Internet, for example, is becoming an important information and marketing tool.

Also, an important trend is to develop tourism in an area in part to promote conservation of the natural environment, historic places and cultural traditions. Ecotourism (controlled nature tourism) and cultural tourism are being developed in many places as a means of justifying and achieving conservation objectives. This is an especially important approach in areas that have limited resources for implementing conservation programmes.

Another fundamental trend internationally is for the commercial facilities and services of tourism to be provided by the private sector, but with government at all levels still being responsible for the overall management of tourism so that it meets national, regional and community environmental and socio-economic objectives. In fact, in some areas, government-owned hotels are now being privatised as part of national policy. However, in some newly developing tourism areas where it is difficult to attract private investment, the government may still need to be the pioneer developer.

CONCEPTS OF SUSTAINABLE TOURISM

As referred to in the Introduction of this guide, the 1987 report, Our Common Future, prepared by the World Commission on Environment and Development for the United Nations defined a sustainable development policy as one that " "meets the needs of the present without compromising the ability of future generations to meet their own needs." At the United Nations Conference on Environment and Development, popularly known as the Earth Summit and held in Rio de Janeiro in 1992, the sustainable development approach was further elaborated and expressed in Agenda 21 that was adopted by the conference. Since then, many national governments have adopted sustainability as their fundamental development policy. The WTO has adopted the sustainable approach to tourism, and applies sustainable development principles in all of its tourism planning and development studies.

The WTO has defined sustainable tourism as follows:
"Sustainable tourism development meets the needs of present tourists and host regions while protecting and enhancing opportunities for the future. It is envisaged as leading to management of all resources in such a way that economic, social, and aesthetic needs can be fulfilled while maintaining cultural integrity, essential ecological processes, biological diversity, and life support systems."

Within the framework of this basic statement, principles of sustainable tourism development can be further elaborated as follows:

- **The natural, historical, cultural and other resources for tourism are conserved for continuous use in the future, while still bringing benefits to the present society.** The sustainable development approach is particularly important in tourism because this sector depends mostly on tourist attractions and activities that are related to the natural environment and historic and cultural heritage of an area. If these resources are degraded or destroyed, then tourism cannot thrive. In fact, conservation of some of these resources can often be enhanced through tourism development. Maintaining the desirable aspects of cultural traditions and ethnic identities is an important element of conserving the cultural heritage of an area. Conservation of tourism resources can help make residents of an area more aware of their heritage and support its protection.

- **Tourism development is planned and managed so that it does not generate serious environmental or sociocultural problems in the tourism area.** Environmental planning approaches and carrying capacity analysis are important techniques for preventing environmental and sociocultural problems resulting from tourism. Application of environmentally friendly technology can greatly assist in reducing the adverse effects of tourism development.

- **The overall environmental quality of the tourism area is maintained and improved where needed.** Most tourists wish to visit areas that are attractive, functional, clean and not polluted. Tourism can provide the incentive and means to maintain and, where needed, improve the environmental quality of areas. A high level of environmental quality is also very important for the local residents to enjoy. Tourism can help make residents more aware of the quality of their environment and support its maintenance and, where necessary, improvement.

- **A high level of tourist satisfaction is maintained so that the tourist destinations will retain their marketability and popularity.** If tourists are not satisfied with the tourism area, it cannot retain its tourist markets and remain as a viable destination. Older resorts, for example, usually require periodic revitalisation to meet present sustainability and marketing objectives.

- **The benefits of tourism are widely spread throughout the society.** Tourism development should be planned and managed so that its socio-economic benefits are spread as widely as possible throughout the society of the tourist destination. In this way, benefits will be maximised and residents will support tourism if they are receiving benefits from it. Community-based tourism projects are an important technique for spreading benefits to local residents.

Also essential is that tourism be politically acceptable without compromising its sustainability. Unless there is political support and commitment to sustainable tourism, tourism plans based on sustainable principles will not be implemented. Sustainable tourism can best be achieved through careful planning, development and management of the tourism sector.

Agenda 21 is a comprehensive programme of action adopted by 182 governments at the Earth Summit in 1992 on major environmental and development issues at the global level. Agenda 21 provides a blueprint for securing the sustainable future of the planet. Within the framework of Agenda 21, the World Tourism Organization, World Travel and Tourism Council and The Earth Council prepared the report, Agenda 21 for the Travel and Tourism Industry: Towards Environmentally Sustainable Development. This programme sets forth the specific role that travel and tourism can play in achieving the objectives of Agenda 21. Agenda 21 for Travel and Tourism states:

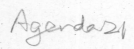

- For government departments, NTAs and representative trade organisations, the overriding aim is to establish systems and procedures to incorporate sustainable development considerations at the core of the decision-making process and to identify actions necessary to bring sustainable tourism development into being.

- For companies, the main aim is to establish systems and procedures to incorporate sustainable development issues as a part of the core management function and to identify actions needed to bring sustainable tourism into being.

Agenda 21 for Travel and Tourism establishes priority areas and actions. Priority Area IV is about planning for sustainable tourism development. Because local authorities have much of the responsibility for the planning and development of tourist attractions, facilities and infrastructure in their areas, this priority is particularly relevant to this guide. **Figure 5** reproduces the Agenda 21 recommendations of Priority Area IV on planning.

Priority Area VI of Agenda 21 deals with providing for the participation of all sectors of society in tourism and is also important to developing tourism in local areas. Emphasis in participation is placed on providing

Figure 5

AGENDA 21 FOR TRAVEL AND TOURISM - PRIORITY AREA IV: PLANNING FOR SUSTAINABLE TOURISM DEVELOPMENT

Objective:
to develop and implement effective land use planning measures that maximise the potential environmental and economic benefits of travel and tourism while minimising potential environmental or cultural damage.

Tourism has huge potential to bring economic prosperity and environmental improvement to the destinations in which it operates. Poorly planned and managed tourism can, however, harm the very resources on which it is based. Environmental and cultural degradation can be avoided by the adoption and enforcement of appropriate planning measures. The organisations addressed in this chapter are ideally placed to advise on the development of such planning measures and to facilitate discussion with all other stakeholders so as to achieve consensus on their enforcement.

In this area, government departments, NTAs and, where appropriate, trade organisations should:

- Work with local and regional planning authorities to raise awareness of the potential problems associated with poor tourism planning and management

- Advise local authorities on the components of a sustainable tourism destination by providing guidance, such as that contained in the World Tourism Organization publication, Sustainable Tourism Development: A Guide for Local Planners

- Guide tourism development in particularly sensitive or protected areas; in some instances, this may include recommending a full environmental impact assessment prior to the full development decision or even advising against any development

- Ensure that planning regulations, measures, or guidelines are implementable and capable of effective policing through voluntary or regulatory means

- Help local and regional authorities to assess destination 'capacity' as regards the availability of critical resources (land, water, energy, infrastructural provision, etc.) environmental factors (ecosystem health and biodiversity), and cultural factors

- In the area of transport:

- develop and promote cost-effective, efficient, less polluting transport systems
- work with local authorities and companies to ensure efficient operation of public transport and maintenance of transport infrastructure

- ensure that new tourism developments are located in areas well served by high-occupancy public transport or where provision of such transport is included as part of the planning proposal

- work with government departments, communities, and travel and tourism companies to provide safe cycleways and footpaths for tourist and resident use and to implement other measures to reduce the need to use private motor vehicles for travel to and within the holiday destination

- devote attention to efficient transport management, especially as regards air and road transport

- integrate land use and transport planning to reduce transport demand

- Ensure that tourism and coastal development are complementary rather than conflicting by advising on the adoption of suitable policies, such as the Global Blue Flag, to conserve and enhance bathing beaches used by tourists

- Use tourism as a tool for socio-economic development and environmental protection in sensitive areas such as coastal zones, mountainous regions, and areas of great biological diversity.

opportunities for all sectors of society equally including women, the young and old and indigenous people in a manner that is appropriate to their society and culture. Agenda 21 further states that achieving maximum involvement of all sectors of society in tourism requires suitable training programmes being available. Annex 2 identifies and elaborates on the other priority areas in Agenda 21 for Travel and Tourism.

LEVELS OF TOURISM PLANNING AND DEVELOPMENT

Tourism planning is carried out at various levels, from the macro or more general level to the local or more detailed level. Each level is focused on particular considerations. Ideally, the macro or more general levels are prepared first and the local level planned within the framework of the more general levels. These levels are described as follows:

International level

Concerned with international transportation services, tour programming that includes more than one country, joint product development such as the Silk Road, the Mayan Route and the Slave Route Project and sometimes joint tourism marketing. International tourism organisations, such as **World Tourism Organization** (WTO) and its regional commissions establish global and regional tourism policies and standards, conduct global level research and encourage co-operation among countries and between the public and private sectors. The International Air Transport Association (IATA) and International Civil Aviation Organisation (ICAO) deal with international air transportation standards and other matters. Regional tourism organisations such as the Pacific Asia Travel Association (PATA), Tourism Council of the South Pacific (TCSP), Caribbean Tourism Organisation (CTO), the tourism unit of the Association of Southeast Asian Nations (ASEAN) and Regional Tourism Organisation of Southern Africa (RETOSA) establish regional policies and programmes and encourage co-operation among their member countries. Tourism trade associations, such as the World Travel and Tourism Council (WTTC) and International Hotel and Restaurant Association (IHRA), establish voluntary standards and quality certification schemes and are concerned with issues related to their areas of commercial interest.

National level

Concerned with national tourism policy, structure planning, international access to the country and the major transportation network within the country, major tourist attractions, major tour programmes, setting national level facility and service standards, establishing standards for and sometimes developing tourism education and training institutes, investment policies, and marketing of tourism and providing information services for the entire country.

Regional level

Often done for states or provinces, the regional level is concerned with regional tourism policy and structure planning, regional tour programmes, regional access and transportation network, sometimes establishing facility and service standards, sometimes setting regional investment policies and handling regional tourism marketing. Initiating and co-ordinating education and training programmes in tourism may be an important function at the regional level.

Local or community level

This level includes tourism planning for local areas of sub-regions, cities, towns, villages, resorts, rural areas and some tourist attraction features. The local or community level of tourism planning is concerned with comprehensive tourism area plans, urban tourism plans, and land use planning for resorts and other tourist facility and attraction areas. Special tourism programmes such as ecotourism and village and rural tourism are carried out at the local level. There may be some education and training for tourism at the local level, some tourism marketing and provision of information services and other management functions.

Site planning level

Site planning refers to planning the specific location of buildings and structures, recreation facilities, conservation and landscape areas, parking and other facilities on the development site. Site planning is carried out at the local level based on the land use plan.

Architectural, landscaping and engineering design level

This is the most detailed level and specifies the precise design of buildings, structures, landscaping, other development on the site and the building and infrastructure engineering. Architectural, landscaping, and engineering design is carried out at the local level based on the site plan.

Tourism planning and development must be integrated among all these levels so that the local development policies and planning reflect the regional level, the regional level reflects the national level and the national level reflects international policies and programmes. However, each level must take initiative in developing its tourism sector.

In addition to comprehensive tourism plans, there can be special studies on certain aspects of tourism. These studies may include, for example, environmental, sociocultural and economic impact analyses, marketing studies, developing specialised types of tourism such as marine tourism, youth tourism and health tourism, product improvement studies, improving handicrafts, developing conference tourism, etc.

This guide is for the local or community level of planning and development, but the local authorities must take into account regional and national policies and plans in their activities, so that there is not duplication of efforts and policies and plans at the various levels reinforce one another.

Questions for Discussion

TOURISM IN YOUR AREA

1. Does any tourism development currently exist in your area? If so, what type of tourism is it?

2. How many international tourists visit the country and region in which your area is located? How important is domestic tourism in your country and region?

3. About how many tourists visit your area?
   From the region in which you are located (domestic tourists)?
   From elsewhere in your country (domestic tourists)?
   From other nearby countries (international tourists)?
   From other countries in the world (international tourists)?

4. Of the major tourism trends listed in this section, which ones do you believe are relevant to the existing and potential tourist markets and tourism development in your area?

5. Has your area adopted any policies for sustainable development of any type of development sectors?

6. Do you consider the present type of economic development in your area to be sustainable or not sustainable?

7. What provisions of Agenda 21 for Travel and Tourism are applicable to your area?

8. If there is any tourism development in your area, is it sustainable or not sustainable?

9. What levels of tourism planning should be carried out in your area?

10. In addition to planning, are there any types of special studies on tourism that you think should be conducted for your area?

AN OVERVIEW

Tourism can bring both benefits and problems to an area. If well planned, developed and managed, tourism generates local jobs and income and provides opportunities for local entrepreneurs to establish tourism enterprises, all of which lead to improved living standards of residents. Tax revenue generated by tourism can be used to improve community facilities and services. Tourism requires improved infrastructure which can be used by residents. Tourism can

tourism in the community

stimulate the expansion of other economic activities such as agriculture, fisheries, manufacturing and crafts production. Tourism also stimulates development of new and improved commercial and cultural facilities which can be used by residents as well as tourists. Tourism can provide the justification and help pay for conservation of local nature areas, archaeological and historic sites, arts, crafts and cultural traditions and overall improvement of environmental quality because these are attractions for tourists.

If not well planned, developed and managed, however, tourism can result in congestion, pollution and other environmental problems. Uncontrolled use by tourists of nature conservation areas and historic sites may lead to their deterioration. Over-commercialisation of cultural traditions can result in degradation of the area's cultural heritage. There may be loss of economic benefits to the local area if it does not maintain control of tourism development. Through careful planning, development and management, the benefits of tourism can be maximised and problems minimised, but some trade-offs are inevitable.

The tourism system must be understood in order to plan tourism. This system is integrated and based on demand and supply factors. The demand factors are international and domestic tourists. The supply components are tourist attractions and activities, accommodation and other tourist facilities and services, transportation and other infrastructure and promotion of tourist markets. The supply side is termed the tourism product. Tourism and the environment are closely related and sustainable tourism development depends on protecting the environmental resources for tourism. The partners for sustainable tourism development are the tourism industry, environment supporters and local community, with some people represented in more than one group.

Each local area that is considering developing or expanding tourism should carefully evaluate its resources for tourism. The resources to assess include all types of existing and potential tourist attractions and activities related to the natural environment, cultural heritage and specialised features such as economic activities, urban places, rural environment, health and medical treatment and religious sites, existing development of tourist facilities and services, transportation and other infrastructure and availability of a trained labour force. In addition, other influencing factors on developing tourism must be evaluated including types of tourist markets, cost and convenience of travelling to the area, competing destinations, community sentiment on developing tourism, degree of public health and safety and political stability of the area.

BENEFITS AND PROBLEMS OF TOURISM FOR LOCAL COMMUNITIES

If carefully planned, developed and managed, tourism can bring substantial benefits to local communities. Some important potential benefits include the following:

- An especially important benefit are new jobs generated by tourism. Tourism particularly can provide employment for young people, women and local ethnic minority groups. Tourism employment is provided not only directly in hotels, restaurants and other tourism enterprises but also in the supplying sectors such as agriculture, fisheries, crafts and manufacturing. In economically depressed areas, the jobs provided by tourism may reduce the out-migration of young people to seek employment elsewhere.

- Tourism development can stimulate the establishment of local tourism enterprises. These provide opportunities for local capital investment, jobs, income, profits made from the enterprises and, more generally, developing a sense of entrepreneurship that may not have existed previously in the area.

- The increased income generated by the new jobs and enterprises in tourism results in improvement of local living standards. If the commercial enterprises are locally owned and managed, the profits they make is also likely to remain in the area.

- Tourism generates local tax revenue that can be used to improve community facilities, services and infrastructure such as schools, medical clinics, libraries, parks and recreation facilities and roads.

- Tourism employees learn new skills and technologies, such as use of computers, which enhance local human resource development. Some of these skills and technologies are transferable to other economic activities.

- Tourism requires that adequate infrastructure, such as roads, water supply, electric power, waste management and telecommunications, be developed. This infrastructure can also be designed to serve local communities so that they receive the benefits of infrastructure improvements. Tourism development can help pay for the cost of improved infrastructure.

- Tourism can provide new markets for local products such as agricultural and fisheries items, arts and handicrafts and manufactured goods and thereby stimulate other local economic sectors. Developing tourist facilities can help support the local construction industry.

- Tourism stimulates development of new and improved retail, recreation and cultural facilities, such as speciality shops and improved shopping districts, parks and recreation, cultural centres and theatres, which local residents as well as tourists can use. Tourism often helps pay for cultural facilities and activities such as theatre performances which local communities could not afford without tourism.

- The overall environmental quality of an area may be improved as a result of tourism because tourists prefer to visit attractive, clean and non-polluted places. Land use and transportation patterns may also be improved because tourism serves as a catalyst for redevelopment of some places.

- Tourism can provide the justification and help pay for conservation of local nature areas, archaeological and historic sites, arts, crafts and certain cultural traditions because these features are the attractions for tourists. Therefore, they must be maintained and often enhanced if tourism is to be successful and sustainable.

- Tourism encourages a greater environmental awareness and sense of cultural identity by residents when they see tourists enjoying the local environmental, historical and cultural heritage. Often residents develop a renewed sense of pride in their heritage when they realise that tourists appreciate it. In this respect, tourism may stimulate revitalisation of certain aspects of the cultural heritage that otherwise are being lost through the forces of modern development.

Figure 6 illustrates how the economic benefits of tourism flow through the local economy. As shown in this diagram, there is some loss of economic benefits to purchasing goods from outside the area while use of locally produced goods and services leads to increased benefits within the local economy. The diagram also shows that some attractions, facilities and services—**parks, s**ports centres, theatres, stores and art and craft galleries— developed for tourism are ones that community residents can also use.

If not well planned, developed and managed, however, tourism can result in problems for the local area.

Some of these potential problems are:

- Traffic and pedestrian congestion and excessive noise levels can result from uncontrolled tourism development. Finding adequate parking

Figure 6

TOURISM AND THE COMMUNITY

When tourists spend money, they create a chain reaction that produces additional economic benfits. They trade with businesses that purchase supplies and services locally or elsewhere. The business, in turn, purchases supplies and services they need to operate and, through successive rounds of purchases, the initial direct expenditures of visitors spread and multiply throughout the local and regional economy. The following chart demonstrates how tourism spending flows through the economy.

spaces for vehicles may become a problem in tourism areas.

- Air pollution can be generated by excessive use of internal combustion vehicles by tourists and tour operators. Construction of tourist facilities may create air pollution on a temporary basis.

- Surface and underground water pollution can result from poor disposal and treatment of sewage and solid waste material. Improper disposal of waste material can also lead to spread of vermin and diseases.

- Tourism areas may become unattractive because of the inappropriate design of tourist facilities, ugly advertising signs and littering by tourists.

- Important tourist attractions such as museums, theatres and parks may be used so much by tourists that local residents cannot have convenient access to these features. This leads to resentment of tourism by residents.

- Uncontrolled use by visitors of nature parks and archaeological and historic sites may lead to their deterioration. Improper viewing of wildlife, for example, may be disruptive to animals' normal behavioural and breeding patterns. Graffiti, vandalism and illegal removal of items as souvenirs may despoil archaeological and historic sites.

- There can be degradation of the local cultural heritage and loss of a sense of cultural identity if there is undue commercialisation and modification of the local arts, crafts and traditions. Imitation of some of the behavioural patterns of tourists by local young people may result in loss of local cultural values and traditions.

- The generation of economic benefits to the local communities and residents may be limited if many persons from outside the area are employed in tourism and tourism enterprises are mostly owned and managed by outsiders. There is also economic loss if most of the products used in tourism are imported from elsewhere although importation of goods and services may be necessary in some places which have few local resources.

Through careful planning, systematic implementation of that planning and continuous effective management of tourism, the benefits can be maximised and problems minimised. However, some trade-offs are inevitable in any type of development including tourism. Each community must decide whether it can maximise benefits, minimise problems and accept the trade-offs of benefits and problems that may result from developing tourism.

THE TOURISM SYSTEM

Tourism should be viewed as an integrated system and socio-economic sector. The functional tourism system is based on supply and demand factors as illustrated in **Figure 7**. The demand factor is comprised of the existing and potential tourist markets, both domestic and international. The supply factors are represented by tourism development of attractions, transportation, facilities and services and the promotion of tourism.

Most types of accommodation, tour and travel services and other tourist facilities and services and some types of tourist attractions typically comprise the commercial private sector of tourism and is often collectively termed the tourism industry. The tourism industry is the heart of the tourism sector—the industry must make the investments in commercial enterprises, manage and operate them efficiently and especially provide good quality services to tourists, and it must be innovative in developing new tourism products in response to tourists' expectations.

Many types of tourist attractions, such as parks and archaeological and historic sites are owned and managed by government agencies although admission fees help pay for the operational cost of these places. Transportation and other infrastructure are typically owned and managed by government or public or private utility corporations, with user fees paying for some of the capital investment and operational costs.

Marketing of the tourist destination and other institutional elements of the tourism system are typically the responsibility of government in co-operation with the private sector. The government's role in facilitating and co-ordinating tourism development is an essential one to achieve the overall tourism development objectives and particularly to bring economic benefits to the community without tourism generating serious environmental, economic or sociocultural problems.

The term used to define the supply side of the tourism system is the tourism product. The tourism product comprises the tourist attractions and activities, accommodation and other tourist facilities and services and the infrastructure that serves the attractions, facilities and services. A key concept in developing a successful tourism sector in an area is to match the tourist markets and the tourism product. The tourism product determines in part the types of tourist markets that can be attracted, and the product must be in suitable form to meet the

Figure 7

THE FUNCTIONAL TOURISM SYSTEM

The functional tourism system. The supply side of tourism (development) should be in balance with demand (markets). Supply is modelled to include five interdependent components:attractions, transportation, services, information, and promotion.

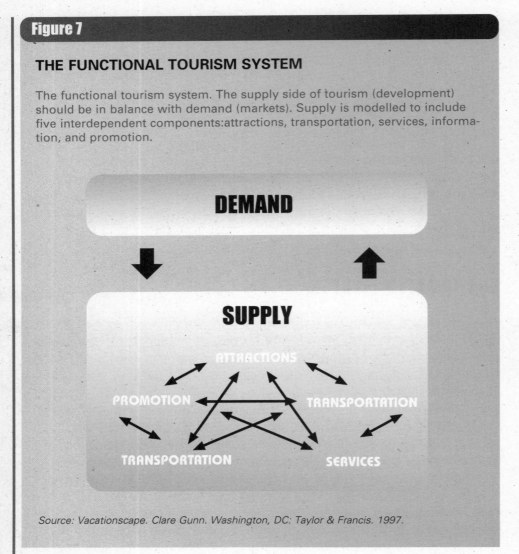

DEMAND

SUPPLY

ATTRACTIONS

PROMOTION   TRANSPORTATION

TRANSPORTATION   SERVICES

Source: Vacationscape. Clare Gunn. Washington, DC: Taylor & Francis. 1997.

tourist markets' expectations. The tourism product, however, must not be developed to match the tourist markets to the extent that it creates local environmental or social problems. Matching the tourist markets and tourism product must be carried within the framework of achieving sustainable and balanced tourism development that optimises benefits to the community.

TOURISM, THE ENVIRONMENT AND THE COMMUNITY

Tourism and the environment are closely interrelated. The natural and built environment provides many of the attractions for tourists and tourism development can have both positive and negative impact on the environment. Sustainable tourism development depends on protecting the environmental resources for tourism.

The partners for sustainable tourism development are the tourism industry—owners and managers of tourism commercial enterprises, the environment supporters—advocates for environmental conservation, and the community—residents, community groups and leaders and the local authorities. Typically some members of the community will also be involved in the tourism industry or be environment supporters. **Figure 8** illustrates the interaction needed among these partners that is necessary to achieve improved quality of life for the community, while still achieving conservation of the environmental resources for tourism and reasonable profits for the tourism industry.

Co-operation among all these partners is essential to achieve successful and sustainable tourism development that improves the local quality of life. In a newly developing tourism area, the local authorities must often take the lead role in achieving this co-operation, and may need to set up mechanisms for effective co-operation. If co-operation is not achieved, tourism may still develop but will generate serious problems and not lead to improved quality of life or be sustainable.

EVALUATING LOCAL RESOURCES FOR TOURISM

Each local area or community that is considering developing tourism, or expanding an existing tourism sector, should carefully evaluate its resources for tourism. This evaluation will help decide whether the area has potential for developing or expanding tourism and, if so, what is the most appropriate type of tourism to develop. This exercise becomes a pre-feasibility study for developing tourism and, if there is development potential, provides the basis for conducting a detailed tourism planning study.

The types of tourism resources to assess in the area are:

Attractions and activities related to the natural environment which can provide opportunities for beach and marine tourism including water sports, snow skiing, nature and ecotourism of wildlife viewing and hiking, controlled fishing and hunting, viewing of special natural features such as waterfalls and caves, adventure tourism such as trekking, rock climbing, mountaineering, white water boating and special interest tourism related to specialised interests of tourists such as bird watching and wild orchid tours. The climate of the area as related to other attraction features should be assessed.

- Attractions and activities related to cultural heritage of the built environment which may provide opportunities for visits to archaeological sites, historic buildings and gardens and entire historic districts, monuments, special historic features such as bridges and industrial sites and re-enactment of historic events and life styles.

- Attractions and activities related to other aspects of cultural heritage of dance, music, drama, traditional dress, cuisine, traditional architecture and villages, performing arts providing opportunities for organising theatre performances, fairs and festivals, production and sales of crafts and speciality items, village tours and development of village tourism.

- Attractions and activities related to economic activities providing for tours of farming and fishing communities, ranches, plantations, artisans' workplaces and modern factories.

- Attractions and activities related to urban places (urban tourism) providing a combination of features for tours of historic places, museums, buildings with interesting architectural styles, monuments, attending theatre performances, night clubs and major sports events, dining in restaurants and shopping. Many urban places and resorts are suitable for development of meeting and conference facilities.

- Attractions and activities related to rural landscapes and life styles providing opportunities for rural tourism of staying in farmhouses, ranches and plantations and participating in activities associated with those places and local fishing, hunting and hiking.

- Attractions and activities related to health, rest and medical treatment of mineral springs, healthy desert and mountain climates and modern,

Figure 8

THE TOURISM INDUSTRY, THE ENVIRONMENT AND THE COMMUNITY

The diagram of common concerns can be used to facilitate a group discussion

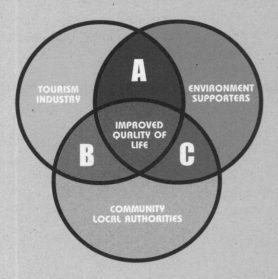

The tourism industry seeks a healthy business environment with:
- financial security
- a trained and responsible workforce

- attractions of sufficient quality to ensure a steady flow of visitors - who stay longer and visit more often

Those interested in natural environment and cultural/heritage issues seek:
- protection of the environment through prevention, improvement, correction of damage, and restoration,
- to motivate people to be more aware - and therefore "care for" rather than "use up" resources

Community members seek a healthy place in which to live with:
- food, adequate and clean water, health care, rewarding work for equitable pay, education and recreation
- respect for cultural traditions
- opportunities to make decisions about the future

Some concerns that each pair may hold in common include:
- issues of access, such as when, where and how tourists visit and move from place to place

- host and guest issues, such as cultural impact or common use of infrastructure

- Land use issues, such as hunting/wildlife habitat, agriculture/recreation, preservation/development, etc.

What issues relate to your community?
How might more groups be involved in the planning and decision-making process?
How might conflicts be resolved so that all viewpoints are honored?

traditional and naturalistic med treatments which provide opportunity for developing he resorts and treatment facilities.

- Specialised attraction featu including scientific and educatic institutions that can be open to public, theme parks, sports fa ties and events and gaming fa ties (gambling casinos), speciali performance themes such as gious plays or specific types music—classical, folk, opera, r jazz, country western, etc.

- Resources related to other form tourism include: important relig sites that attract pilgrims; pla from where there was much m tion of people to other places in past that can provide the basis 'roots' tourism of tourists vis their family and ancestral ho lands; places where persons p ously fought in wars, worked or s ied that can be developed for 'nc gic' tourism.

- The overall environmental qu of the area can be an impor supplementary attraction tourists. Environmental quality ments include the levels of water and noise pollution and gestion, cleanliness of the e ronment, attractiveness and m tenance of buildings, extent maintenance of landscaping e cially in public areas, amoun parks, recreation and open sp appropriate use of water featu pedestrianization of shop areas, night lighting of stre availability of public transporta availability of public toilets, cor of crime and other elements.

- Existing development of to facilities and services such hotels and other types of acc modation, restaurants, tour travel services, tourist informa services, shopping and other types of tourist facilities and services. Often older hotels can be renovated to serve modern tourism and historic hotels can be restored as attractions as well as accommodation for tourists.

- Existing development of transportation access to and within the area and other infrastructure of water supply, electric power supply, waste management and telecommunications.

- Availability of a qualified or trainable labour supply to work in all aspects of tourism. Often a reason for developing tourism is to provide local employment, but training is usually required to provide qualified tourism personnel.

In addition to examining the types of resources listed above, other factors must be evaluated. These include:

- Any existing tourist markets and the major potential international and domestic tourist markets, and whether the potential markets will have an interest in the types of tourist attractions the area can offer. Residents' use of tourist attractions, facilities and services should also be considered.

- The cost and convenience of the potential tourist markets travelling to the destination and the cost for tourists of staying in the area (if some tourism development currently exists). Tourists often select their tourist destinations based on travel cost and convenience factors as well as the quality of attractions, facilities and services.

- Any existing or planned tourism development in other areas that may present competition for the same tourist markets.

- The compatibility of tourism development with other economic activities which exist in the area or have potential for development.

- The recommendations for the area in any existing national or regional tourism development policies and plans.

- The general community sentiment on whether tourism should be developed based on consideration of its benefits and possible problems.

- Existing local government and private sector organisational structures for developing tourism, any existing regulations related to tourism, local financial capacities to invest in tourism development, and any existing training institutions and programmes to produce qualified personnel to work in tourism. All of these factors can be improved over time, if necessary, and recommendations for improvement are typically made during the tourism planning process.

- Public safety and crime level of the area, possibility of terrorist acts against tourists and the degree of political stability that prevails in the local area or country or region, and the effect that these factors may have on attracting tourists. These factors will often change over time.

- Public health, especially related to the level of sanitation and hygiene, and the possibility of disease epidemics in the area. These are factors, however, that can be improved over time if necessary.

Evaluation of the tourism resources and other influencing factors on tourism will provide the basis for deciding whether the area has potential for developing tourism. It will also indicate the types and extent of tourism that the area could develop. If this 'pre-feasibility' evaluation is generally positive indicating that tourism can desirably be developed, then the area can proceed with detailed planning for tourism.

If the area does not have adequate resources for developing tourism or there are major constraints on development such as difficult access, then a realistic decision should be made not to develop tourism at least at the present time. It would be a waste of financial and administrative resources to attempt to develop tourism that would not likely be successful. Other economic sectors can be examined for their development potential.

SURVEY OF LOCAL RESOURCES FOR DEVELOPING TOURISM

This checklist can be used for a preliminary survey of tourism resources in your local area or community and surrounding region. Complete all of the categories that apply and leave the others blank. You may need to add some additional categories depending on the particular resources existing in your area. This is only a preliminary overview in order to determine the potential for tourism and types of tourism that can be developed. A detailed resource survey and analysis would be carried out as part of the planning process explained in the next section.

Natural resources

- beaches ....
- marine environment (coral reefs, game fish, etc.) ....
- mountain recreation and scenery ....
- deserts ....
- forests ....
- waterfalls ....
- lakes ....
- caves ....
- wildlife including birdlife ....
- mineral & hot springs ....
- designated protected areas (parks & reserves) ....
- other types ....

Archaeological, historic, cultural resources

- archaeological sites ....
- historic towns, urban districts and buildings ....
- traditional villages and architecture ....
- folklore & traditional medicine ....
- traditional dress & customs ....
- festivals & ceremonies
- traditional crafts & craft villages ....
- traditional and modern economic activities ....
- traditional and modern performing arts (dance, music, drama)........
- museums of all types ....
- cultural facilities & centres ....
- scientific and educational centres ....
- rural landscapes & settlements ....
- other ....

Special types of attractions

- major sports events and facilities ....
- evening entertainment ....
- theme parks ....
- zoos and botanical gardens ....
- gambling casinos ....
- other types ....

Climate

	average annual	seasonal distribution
temperature	....	....
rainfall	....	....
relative humidity	....	....
sunny days	....	....
prevailing winds	....	....

Environmental quality

	good	moderate	poor
air quality	....	....	....
water quality	....	....	....
cleanliness of environment	....	....	....
attractiveness of environment	....	....	....
maintenance of buildings & public spaces	....	....	....
congestion	....	....	....
other factors	....	....	....

Infrastructure

- transportation access to the area
  air ....
  water ....
  roads ....
  railway ....
- transportation within the area (all types) ....
- water supply ....
- electric power ....
- waste management - sewage ....
- waste management - solid waste ....
- telecommunications ....
- postal ....
- other (drainage, etc.) ....

Tourist facilities and services

- accommodation by type, size and number of rooms ....
- restaurants by type and quality ....
- tour and travel services ....
- tour guides ....
- shopping (craft, speciality, convenience) ....
- tourist information services ....
- banking & money exchange ....
- medical facilities & services ....
- police protection services ....
- other facilities & services

Human resource development (HRD)

- qualifications of present employees in tourism ....
- existing training facilities & programmes in tourism ....
- future availability of qualified labour force ....
- other HRD considerations ....

Influencing factors on developing tourism

- existing and potential tourist markets ....
- cost & convenience of travel to area ....
- competing destinations ....
- community sentiment on tourism ....
- organisational and financial capacities ....
- political stability ....
- public safety and security ....
- public health, sanitation & hygiene ....
- other influencing factors ....

AN OVERVIEW

Planning for tourism is aimed at bringing certain socio-economic benefits to society while maintaining sustainability of the tourism sector through protecting the environment and local culture. Planning is prepared within a time framework and must apply a flexible, comprehensive, integrated, environmental and sustainable, community-based and implementable approach.

planning for local tourism development

SECTION

3

The strategic planning approach is sometimes applicable. All the components of tourism must be considered in planning: tourist attractions and activities, accommodation, other tourist facilities and services, transportation, other infrastructure and the institutional elements.

Tourism planning is carried out according to a systematic process of sequential steps:

- Study preparation including writing the terms of reference for the planning project.

- Determination of tourism development objectives.

- Surveys and evaluation of all the relevant elements.

- Analysis and synthesis of the survey information.

- Formulation of the tourism policy and plan.

- Formulation of other recommendations.

- Implementation and management.

Planning for development of specific tourism projects must also be carried out in a systematic manner based on sequential steps of project identification, screening, planning and feasibility analysis, development organisation, funding, implementation and management. The environmental impact assessment (EIA) procedure must be applied to tourism projects to give greater assurance that they will bring benefits to the area and not generate serious environmental or socio-economic problems.

Local authorities must determine and adopt site planning principles, development standards and design guidelines for tourist facilities so that they are integrated into the environment and do not generate environmental problems. Development standards relate to several factors: densities, building height limits and setbacks, site coverage, landscaping, off-street parking, sign controls, public access, undergrounding of utility lines and others. In coastal areas, requiring adequate setbacks of buildings from the shoreline is essential. Appropriate architectural, landscaping and engineering design of facilities is very important. Quality standards for tourist facilities and services must be adopted and properly administered to ensure that facilities are of acceptable standard and meet the expectations of tourists.

PLANNING APPROACHES

Planning is organising the future to achieve certain objectives. It provides a guide for decision-making on appropriate future actions. Planning for tourism is aimed at bringing certain socio-economic benefits to society while maintaining sustainability of the tourism sector. Tourism planning may be incorporated into the general planning for an area and, if this can be accomplished, tourism will automatically be integrated into the area's development patterns. However, the more typical situation is that the tourism plan is prepared separately because it is needed to guide development as soon as possible after the decision has been made to develop tourism, or to improve and expand existing tourism development.

Plans are usually prepared for a specified time period so that there is a time framework for establishing development targets and monitoring the progress of tourism. Typically, plans will be prepared for a long-term period of about 15 years, but this can range from 10 to 20 years. The end of the planning period is termed the horizon year of the plan. Within the long-term time planning period, recommendations are made for development projects and actions that should be carried out during the short- or near-term period of the first five years of the plan. Some local authorities may consider the short-term period to be only two to three years. Recommendations may also be made for the medium-term period of five to ten years.

There are several basic tourism planning approaches, applied in combination, which underlay the planning process. These are:

Continuous and flexible approach

The plan should be responsive to changing circumstances, but any modifications needed should be made within the framework of achieving the development objectives and concepts of sustainable tourism. Usually, the near-term recommendations are specific to provide precise guidance for near-term development, while longer-term recommendations are more general and will be specified later based on circumstances prevailing at that time.

Comprehensive approach

All aspects of tourism development must be considered in the planning process. These are the components described in the tourism system: tourist attractions and activities, accommodation, other tourist facilities and services, transportation, other infrastructure and the institutional elements.

Integrated approach

Tourism is integrated as a system in itself, and the tourism sector is integrated into the overall development policies and plans of the area, and local plans are integrated into the national and regional tourism policies and plans.

Environmental and sustainable approach

Tourism is planned in an environmentally sensitive manner so that its natural and cultural resources are conserved, tourism development does not generate serious adverse environmental or sociocultural impacts, the overall environmental quality of the area is maintained or improved, the benefits of tourism are widely spread in the society and tourist satisfaction levels are sustained.

Community-based approach

To the extent possible, there should be maximum involvement of local communities in the planning and development of tourism, with benefits accruing to the local communities including minority and disadvantaged groups.

Implementable approach

Tourism is planned so that development can realistically be implemented and implementation techniques are considered throughout the planning process. Planning must also apply contemporary and creative concepts of development. Political realities must be considered but long-term development objectives and policies should not be compromised.

The strategic planning approach

is sometimes appropriate. Strategic planning focuses more on identification and resolution of immediate issues. It is typically used in a rapidly changing situation, is action oriented and emphasises how to cope with changes organisationally. It is less comprehensive than the long-term planning described above, but may be effectively used within the framework of long-term policy and planning. For example, a long-term comprehensive plan often includes a short to medium term action programme as a technique of implementation.

COMPONENTS OF TOURISM PLANNING

The tourism sector is comprised of several different components which must be understood and carefully planned and developed in an integrated manner if tourism is to be successfully developed in a community. For the convenience of planning tourism in a community, these components are organised as shown in **Figure 9** and described below.

Figure 9

COMPONENTS OF A TOURISM PLAN

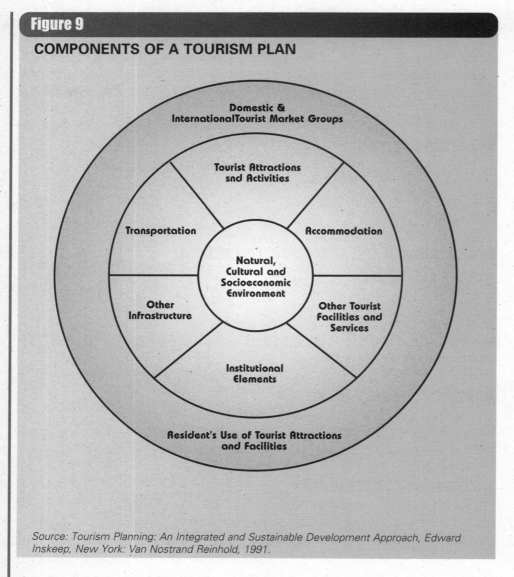

Source: Tourism Planning: An Integrated and Sustainable Development Approach, Edward Inskeep, New York: Van Nostrand Reinhold, 1991.

Tourist markets

There must be existing or potential tourists (the tourist markets) to visit the area. These markets may be international, national (domestic) or from the local region and are often a combination of these types. Some markets may be general interest tourists while others have special interests they are seeking to satisfy. Tourist markets include business travellers. Local residents' use of tourist attractions, facilities, services and infrastructure must also be considered in developing tourism.

Tourist attractions and activities

Attractions and activities must be available to induce tourists to visit the area. Attractions can be natural such as nature parks and beach/marine areas, archaeological sites and historic places, cultural features such as arts and entertainment, crafts, traditional architectural styles, economic activities, traditional customs and ceremonies and 'man-made' features such as theme parks and casinos and special events such as fairs, festivals and sports competitions. Many types of features can be developed as tourist attractions.

Accommodation

Hotels and other types of facilities where tourists can stay overnight must be provided. Accommodation also often contains restaurants and other tourist facilities. Sometimes historic or unusual types of accommodation may be attractions in themselves. Without accommodation, tourists can only visit the area on day tours. However, for some local communities day tours may still generate some benefits.

Other tourist facilities and services

Tour and travel services are necessary to make travel arrangements for tourists and provide guide services. Providing tourist information facilities and services in the area is very important. Other tourist facilities and services include restaurants and other types of eating and drinking establishments, postal facilities and services, medical facilities and services for tourists who experience medical problems while travelling, banking and money exchange, retail shops that handle convenience items, crafts and souvenirs, art galleries and antique shops and often speciality items such as designer clothes, personal services such as hair dressing, and other types. Providing adequate public safety in the tourism area is essential to protect the tourists from criminal or terrorist acts. Proper public health measures to prevent environmentally-based diseases must also be maintained.

Transportation

Adequate transportation access to the tourism area and a functional transportation network to serve attractions and tourist facilities in the area are essential. Transportation can be by air, land (road and rail) and water (ocean, lake, river). Transportation includes both facilities and services such as aircraft, train and bus capacities, routes and schedules and efficiency of the services provided.

Other infrastructure

Other infrastructure required to serve tourism and tourist facilities include hygienic water supply, adequate electric power, proper waste management (sewage and solid waste collection, treatment and disposal) and adequate telecommunications. Sometimes these can be provided on the sites of the tourist facilities by the facility operators, but typically must be provided by the local authorities or utility companies.

Institutional elements

Several institutional type elements are necessary for developing and managing tourism. These include education and training of persons to work effectively in tourism (human resource development), marketing and promotion of the tourist destination and its attractions and facilities, standards and regulatory mechanisms for tourist facilities and services including land use and environmental controls, and often financial mechanisms to encourage investment in tourism development. Organisational structures for tourism are essential and include both government tourism agencies and boards and associations of private tourism enterprises.

Tourism planning at any level must consider all these components in order to be comprehensive and integrated.

TOURISM PLANNING PROCESS

Tourism planning must be carried out according to a systematic process in order to be effective. The planning process varies somewhat depending on the type of planning and local conditions, but it generally follows these steps:

- **Study Preparation**
- **Determination of Development Objectives**
- **Surveys and Evaluations**
- **Analysis and Synthesis**
- **Policy and Plan Formulation**

- **Recommendations**
- **Implementation and Management**

The steps in the planning process are explained below.

1. Study preparation

The pre-feasibility study (evaluation of resources) is completed and, if the evaluation is positive, the decision is made by the local authorities to proceed with tourism planning. Next the terms of reference (TOR) of the planning study project are prepared. The TOR must be carefully written so that the planning project is properly carried out and achieves the desired results. Then the project team is selected. For a comprehensive study, a multi-disciplinary team is required that includes specialists on physical planning, marketing, economic and financial analysis, environmental and sociocultural considerations and infrastructure planning. Depending on the type of tourism area, other specialists may be needed such as on mountain trekking and marine sports.

2. Determination of tourism development objectives

The objectives state what is expected to be achieved through tourism development. Objectives typically combine and balance economic, environmental and sociocultural factors and should always include the concept of sustainability. These are determined in a preliminary manner at the start of the project and later refined based on feedback during the planning process. The objectives should be determined in close coordination with community residents and their leaders, as well as the government authorities.

3. Surveys and evaluations

Surveys are conducted and evaluations made of the many elements related to tourism in the area. These elements include:

- Characteristics of the area's environmental, economic, sociocultural, land use and land tenure patterns. Special considerations such as land tenure which affects the availability of land for development should be highlighted in this background analysis.

- Tourism resources of existing and potential tourist attractions and activities. Evaluation of tourism resources must include accessibility to attraction sites. The overall environmental quality of the area should also be evaluated.

- Existing tourism development including accommodation and other tourist facilities and services. The quality level of existing tourist facilities and services is important to evaluate.

- Existing and potential tourist markets and travel patterns. If there is some existing tourism, a special survey should be conducted of tourist arrivals to determine their characteristics and attitudes toward existing tourist attractions, activities, facilities and services and their expenditure patterns in the area.

- Existing and already planned transportation access to and within the area including air, road and rail and water transportation. Both transportation facilities and services should be surveyed including frequencies and capacities of transportation carriers.

- Other types of existing and already planned infrastructure including water supply, electric power, waste management and telecommunications.

- Present development policies and plans of the area, region and country including both overall development policies and plans and those adopted for tourism.

- Institutional elements of tourism including availability of a qualified labour force to work in tourism and any existing tourism education and training programmes, public and private organisational structures for tourism, tourism-related laws and regulations including tourist facility standards, land use controls and environmental protection, and financial capital available for investment in tourism and any financial mechanisms adopted to attract investment.

Tourist attractions are specifically inventoried, categorised and evaluated. They are categorised into types of attractions related to the natural, historic and cultural heritage and specialised features. They are usually identified as primary attractions—features that may induce tourists to visit the area, and secondary attractions—features that complement the primary attractions and may induce tourists to stay longer in the area. Other influencing factors on tourism such as political stability, public health and safety and effect of competing destinations must be evaluated as described in Section 2.

Figure 10 is a Model Tourism Resource Survey Form that can be used for description and evaluation of specific resource features. **Figure 11** presents a checklist for identifying the tourism potential of a protected area attraction such as a nature park. Tourism, and especially ecotourism, in a local area can often be developed based on an existing protected area. If natural and historic/cultural attractions are limited, consideration can be given to the feasibility of developing specialised types of attraction features such as theme parks, ideally related to the indigenous culture, local historical features and /or the natural environment of the area.

4. Analysis and synthesis

All the elements surveyed are analysed in an integrated and comprehensive manner (planning synthesis) to understand their inter-relationships. It is important to carefully analyse tourist markets in relation to the types of attractions and activities that can be available for tourists and other components of the tourism product. Instead of projecting tourist arrivals, which is difficult if there is little or no existing tourism in the area, the approach is used of establishing market targets. These targets indicate the number and types of tourists that can be attracted to the area if the recommendations of the tourism plan, such as improvements to attractions, facilities, services, transportation and other infrastructure and promotional programmes, are implemented. Establishing market targets

Figure 10

TOURISM RESOURCE SURVEY FORM

This worksheet can be used for a preliminary inventory of each natural, cultural, historical and recreational tourism resource which can attract tourists to the community or region.

Name of resource: ....

Location: ....

Type and description: ....
- Present condition ....
- Improvements planned ....
- Improvements needed ....

Special features: ....

....

When is the resource accessible to tourists? ....

During the year? ....

During the week? ....

Who visits now? Identify type of visitor, place of origin and seasonal volume. ....

....

What transportation is available between this resource and the tourist's place of origin? ....

Domestic ....

International ....

Where do international tourists enter the country? ....

What other tourism services and facilities exist at the site now? ....

....

Name of service or facility ....

Name of owner ....

Address ....

Phone ....

Who is responsible for:

Development ....

Conservation ....

Promotion ....

What other resources are nearby? ....

....

Is this resource on the itinerary of any tours? (explain) ....

....

....

Briefly evaluate this resource

For its attractiveness ....

....

For its carrying capacity ....

....

For its compatibility with regional and national plans..

....

Source: World Tourism Organization.

Figure 11

CHECKLIST FOR IDENTIFYING THE TOURISM POTENTIAL OF A PROTECTED AREA

In many countries, there is a symbiotic relationship between tourism and the establishment of protected areas. When this occurs, the tourist potential in the surrounding area is then an important factor in the selection process. Statistics show that growing numbers of vacationers and holiday seekers want to see something different. They want to travel in relative comfort. And they want to mix adventure, and possibly learning, with leisure activities. Consequently, the most successful tourist packages combine a number of different interests: sports and recreation, wildlife viewing, becoming acquainted with local customs, visiting historical sites, photographing or sketching spectacular scenes shopping, eating, and, most of all, water activities. The sea, lakes, rivers, swimming pools, and waterfalls all have high value, particularly for domestic tourism.

The following questions will help evaluate the tourist potential surrounding a protected area:

Is the protected area
- close to an international airport or major tourist centre
- moderately close
- remote

Is the journey to the area
- easy and comfortable
- some effort
- difficult or dangerous

Is successful wildlife viewing
- guaranteed
- usual
- only available with luck or highly seasonal

Does the area offer
- several distinctive features of interest
- more than one feature of interest
- one main feature of interest

Does the area offer
- many additional cultural interests
- some additional cultural attractions
- few cultural attractions

Is the area
- unique in its appeal
- somewhat different
- similar to other\visitor reserves

Does the area have
- beach or lakeside recreation facilities
- river, falls or swimming pools
- no water-related recreation

Is the area close enough to other sites of tourist interest to be part of a tourist circuit?
- yes
- moderate potential
- Low or no potential

Is the surrounding area
- of high scenic beauty
- moderately attractive
- rather ordinary

What standards of food are available?
- varied and well prepared
- adequate
- basic

What standards of lodging accommodations are available?
- varied and comfortable
- adequate
- primitive

Source: Managing Protected Areas in the Tropics, MacKinnon et al., IUCN, Gland, Switzerland.

Figure 12

PROJECTING ACCOMMODATION NEEDS

The formula for projecting accommodation needs, and an example for determining average annual and high season demand, are set forth below. This example is only for one type of tourist market and accommodation. The formula should be applied to each of the tourist markets and related types of accommodation to determine the total accommodation for the area. Calculating high season demand is important because that season determines the maximum needs.

Demand for beds

The formula is:

No. of tourists per time period X average length of stay in nights
No. of nights per time period X accommodation occupancy factor

For example, to calculate annual beds demand:

100,000 tourists per year X 10 nights = 1,000,000 = 3,650 beds
365 nights x 75% occupancy = 274

For example, to calculate high season beds demand:

50,000 tourists per 4 months X 10 nights = 500,000 = 4,386 beds
120 nights X 95% occupancy = 114

Demand for rooms

The formula is:

No. of beds demand
Average room occupancy (persons per room)

For example, to calculate annual rooms demand:

3,650 beds = 2,147 rooms
1.7 persons per room

For example, to calculate high season rooms demand:

4,386 beds = 2,580 rooms
1.7 persons per room

Allowance should be made for the percentage of tourists who stay in non-commercial accommodation such as with friends and relatives. If this factor is, for example, 5 per cent, that percentage should be deducted from the calculated bed and room demand. If there is a strong seasonality factor as indicated in this example, a decision must be made whether to provide sufficient accommodation to handle all the high season demand which will reduce the average annual occupancy, or to not accommodate all the high season demand in order to maintain higher average annual occupancies. The best approach is to use techniques to reduce the seasonality factor of demand.

should include the average length of stay of tourists.

The market targets provide the basis for calculating the tourist accommodation needed, as shown in **Figure 12**, as well as needs for other types of tourist facilities and services and tourism infrastructure. The targets are also used for projecting the economic impact of tourism in the future, based on the projected expenditure patterns of tourists.

A basic environmental planning technique is carrying capacity analysis. This is not a precise tool but provides a very useful guideline to determine the optimum level of development and use of attraction features, facilities and services. Establishing carrying capacities is based on the concept of maintaining a level of tourism development or visitor use of a site that will:

- Not result in serious environmental deterioration or sociocultural or economic problems in the tourism area.

- Not be perceived by tourists as depreciating their enjoyment of the area.

It must be noted that the carrying capacity concept is a relative and not an absolute indicator. Thus, for example, two beaches of similar physical characteristics may have a different carrying capacity depending on the markets they are aimed for and on the level and type of tourist facilities and infrastructure already existing in each of them.

All development results in some changes to the environment but a reasonable and realistic approach is based on not exceeding the levels of acceptable change so that tourism resources are conserved and successful tourism development is sustained. Seasonality is a major consideration with saturation, of course, more likely to be reached (or exceeded) during the peak season. Carrying capacity analysis involves consideration of physical, economic, sociocultural and infrastructure factors as related to impact on the community and impact on the tourists. Annex 3 explains carrying capacity analysis in more detail.

At this stage in the planning process, it is useful to summarise the major opportunities and constraints for developing tourism. This provides the basis for focusing recommendations on taking advantage of development opportunities and resolving or mitigating the development constraints. SWOT analysis is sometimes an effective technique to summarise major opportunities and constraints, especially in strategic planning. In analysing an area's potential for tourism development, SWOT refers to identification of:

- Strengths

- Weaknesses

- Opportunities

- Threats

The factors identified under each of these categories are expressed in a series of short statements which can then be easily compared to make a summary analysis of the area's potential for developing tourism. They also provide the basis for formulating the priority recommendations for development.

Figure 13

SAMPLE MATRIX FOR EVALUATING ALTERNATIVE PLANS

EVALUATION FACTOR	EVALUATION RANKING			
	ALTERNATIVE 1	ALTERNATIVE 2	ALTERNATIVE 3	COMMENTS
Reflects overall national/regional/local development policy				
Reflects national/regional/local tourism policy and objectives				
Optimizes overall economic benefits at reasonable cost				
Provides substantial employment and increased income to local communities				
Provides opportunity for local entrepreneurs to establish tourism enterprises				
Helps develop economically depressed areas				
Provides tourist attractions, facilities and services which residents can also use				
Does not preempt other important resources areas				
Minimizes negative sociocultural impacts				
Helps achieve archaeological/historic preservation				
Helps revitalize traditional arts and handicrafts				
Is not disruptive to present land use and settlement patterns				
Minimizes negative environmental Impacts				
Reinforces environmental conservation & park development				
Makes maximum use of existing infrastructure				
Makes maximum multi-purpose use of new infrastructure				
Provides opportunity for staging development				

Notes:

1. This list of evaluation factors is only an example of the type which could be used, and the evaluation factors actually used will depend on the specific planning situation. If the plan objectives are complete and specific they can sometimes be used directly as the factors.

2. The evaluation ranking can be done on a scale of 1 to 5 or 1 to 10 with the upper end of the scale indicating the higher achievement level. The more important factors can be given a greater numerical weighting. The comments column is important for noting special situations. Foe example, substantial employment may be provided by the plan but considerable migration of workers may be required to provide employment.

Source: Tourism Planning: An Integrated and Sustainable Development Approach, Edward Inskeep. New York: Van Nostrand Reinhold, 1991.

5. Policy and plan formulation

Based on the objectives, surveys, analysis and synthesis, the tourism development policy is formulated and the tourism physical plan is prepared. Tourism policy states the extent and type of tourism development and special considerations such as economic, environmental and sociocultural aspects. Annex 4 presents a model municipal tourism policy that can be used as a guide for formulating policy. At the local planning level, the physical plan may be an area-wide structure plan that identifies the main access points to the area, the primary and secondary tourist attractions, the tourism development sites and the transportation network that connects the access to the attraction features and development sites. Or the physical plan may be an urban tourism structure plan, a resort land use plan or the land use plan for tourist facilities at a natural or historic attraction site.

Typically, alternative plans are prepared and evaluated as a basis for selecting the final plan that optimises benefits and minimises problems. **Figure 13** provides a model matrix that can be used to evaluate alternative plans. Sometimes, parts of different alternative plans are combined to determine the optimum final plan. An essential consideration in evaluating alternative plans are environmental and sociocultural impacts, with the plan selected that will likely result in the least negative impacts.

6. Recommendations on the plan elements

Recommendations are made on improvements needed to tourist attractions, existing tourist facilities and services, institutional and other elements of the plan. Development and design standards for tourist facilities are recommended. Environmental and sociocultural impacts are analysed and protection measures recommended, and the economic impact of tourism is analysed and ways recommended to enhance economic benefits.

7. Implementation and management

Plans have little value unless they are capable of being implemented, and are actually implemented. Techniques of implementation should be considered throughout the planning process and specific implementation techniques identified in the planning programme. These techniques include development programming, applying tourist facility standards, zoning regulations, financial mechanisms and other means. Implementation techniques are elaborated in Section 5 of this guide. The continuous effective management of the tourism sector, described in Section 7, is essential to sustain successful development of this sector.

An essential element of the planning process is community participation in the crucial steps of planning and the implementation and management of tourism development. Community participation ensures that the knowledge of community residents about their own areas are incorporated in the surveys and analyses, and that the aspirations of the community for their future development are integrated into determination of development objectives, policies and plan recommendations.

For specific tourism planning projects, a common approach is to establish a project steering committee. This committee is typically comprised of representatives of the involved government agencies, the tourism private sector and community leaders. Other relevant representatives, such as traditional and religious organisations and NGOs (non-governmental organisations) may be included in the committee. This group offers guidance on the planning team's activities and especially discusses the conclusions and recommendations of the team, including review of the draft planning reports.

It is also important to hold public meetings on the draft reports in the planning area communities so that local residents and their spokesmen can be exposed to the planning recommendations and have the opportunity to respond to the recommendations. Public media of local radio, television, newspapers and magazines can also be utilised to disseminate information about the planning. Community involvement in the planning process not only elicits local comment on the recommendations but additionally educates residents about the plan and gains their support of it.

Area-wide plans and other larger-scale plans should include logical staging of development to provide the basis for incremental development over several years. Usually not all recommended development will be needed or can feasibly be developed during the near-term period. Staging is usually for five-year periods with the first stage more specifically planned and programmed, and later stages left more general to be specified at a later time based on circumstances prevailing at that time. As is explained in Section 5 on implementation, a tourism action programme is usually prepared for the first stage of development. After several years have passed, the plan should be reviewed and revisions made if necessary based on changing circumstances and perhaps a shifting of development objectives. However, any revisions must be made within the framework of maintaining the sustainability of tourism.

PROJECT DEVELOPMENT PROCESS

The effective development of specific projects, such as for hotels, resorts and tourist attractions, is an important aspect of planning. This is a specialised subject but, in general terms, the process follows these steps:

Step 1 -
Project identification
Identification of the project is preferably done as part of the comprehensive tourism development plan and programme for the area. In the absence of an area plan, the project can be identified independently but still within the context of overall tourism development patterns in the area.

Step 2 -
Project screening
This step involves conceptual planning and pre-feasibility analysis of the project and determines whether the proposed project is likely to be feasible. If it is determined unfeasible, then it is dropped and another type of project is considered.

Step 3 - Project planning and feasibility analysis
The detailed planning and design and the market, economic and financial feasibility analysis of the project is prepared, with an environmental and social impact assessment made. If the project is determined unfeasible or will generate unacceptable environmental or social impacts, then it is dropped or substantially modified.

Step 4 - Project organisation

The organisational approach to developing the project is determined. An existing organisational structure, whether public or private, can sometimes be used or a new organisation, such as a public or private development corporation, may be the most appropriate approach.

Step 5 -
Project funding

The source of development funding is secured. This may require promotion of the project and provision of investment incentives, and then mobilisation of funds.

Step 6 -
Project implementation

The actual physical development of the project is carried out and personnel are recruited and trained to work in the facilities.

Step 7 -
Project management

Management of the project is a continuous process and includes promotion to tourist markets and proper maintenance of facilities.

Throughout the project development and management process, close co-ordination should be maintained with the local communities. This co-ordination is important to ensure that residents understand the project concept, plan and development programme and agree with it. Especially crucial is that the communities have the opportunity to benefit from the project.

ENVIRONMENTAL IMPACT ASSESSMENT OF TOURISM PROJECTS

Application of the environmental planning approach and incorporation of environmental protection measures into the planning process will prevent many environmental problems from arising. However, it is still important that an environmental impact assessment (EIA) be conducted for each specific tourism development project (and for other types of development projects). The EIA examines a proposed development project with respect to its possible environmental impacts, including socio-cultural and economic impacts, to ensure that no serious negative impacts are likely to result from the development. If such impacts seem likely to occur, then the project will need to be redesigned to prevent them, or else be abandoned. Even though a project may generate substantial economic benefits, for example, it may result in unacceptable environmental or social problems, and therefore should not be approved without modification.

Most countries or regions have adopted environmental protection legislation and the EIA procedure. If the local area does not have an EIA procedure established, however, then it should adopt one that is appropriate for the area. There are many models of the EIA procedure available internationally.

DEVELOPMENT AND DESIGN STANDARDS FOR TOURIST FACILITIES

An essential aspect of local planning for tourism is ensuring that tourist facilities including hotels and resorts, restaurants and visitor facilities at tourist attractions are appropriately sited and designed. These standards and guidelines determine, to a large extent, the physical character of the facilities and their immediate environment and the extent to which the tourism development is integrated into the natural and cultural environment. They also help prevent many types of environmental problems that might result from the development of tourism. They influence both the satisfaction levels of tourists and the overall quality and character of the environment for residents.

Establishing and applying suitable development standards and design guidelines are therefore necessary to guide facility development. This level of planning is carried out by site planners, architects, landscape architects (landscapers) and various types of engineers. Local authorities, however, must establish the standards and guidelines and additionally review the development proposals to ensure that the standards and guidelines have been properly applied. Development and design standards are typically incorporated into local regulations including zoning and architectural controls. In some countries, these standards are established by the national or regional governments. Where local zoning regulations do not exist, the development and design standards can be adopted separately by the local authorities or included in tourism plans that have been adopted. Development and design standards are described in the following sections.

Site planning

which indicates the precise location of buildings and other structures and landscape/conservation areas on a development site, involves several basic considerations:

- Avoiding environmental hazards to the facilities themselves or to the local environment. Particularly hazardous situations are land slippage, especially in building on hillsides with unstable soil conditions, and flooding in low-lying and swampy areas. Development situated close to beaches and coastlines can often be dangerous also, because of the possibility of high waves and coastal erosion. Places which are prone to high winds, volcanic eruptions and earthquakes can present serious hazards to development. Very hazardous areas should not be developed at all and placed in a conservation zone. Less hazardous areas must be carefully developed with appropriate site planning, development standards and building construction techniques.

- Maintaining suitable relationships among the buildings and groupings of buildings on the site, together with recreation, landscaped and conservation areas. This refers to the layout of the buildings and other uses of the site.

- Maintaining view planes and corridors toward visual amenity features. Maintaining view planes refers to not obstructing views above a certain height level. Maintaining view corridors refers to keeping clear views between buildings and other structures. The visual amenity features of a site may include attractive beaches, coastal and water views and mountain scenic beauty.

Development standards

are applicable to the controlled development of tourist facilities. The types of development standards normally used throughout the world for tourist facilities and other kinds of development are:

- **Density of development** which determines much of the character of the tourism site. Density for hotels is expressed in the number of rooms per acre or hectare. Low density implies cottage and single-storey buildings with much landscaping. A low to medium density usually requires two-storey buildings still with much landscaping. Medium to higher density indicates buildings of about four stories with considerable landscaping, and high density refers to taller buildings with limited amount of land-scaping. Ecotourism accommodation, for example, would be of low density. Smaller resorts often have a low to medium density. Many larger resorts, for example, are of medium-higher levels of density so that there is a sufficient amount of area for recreation facilities and landscaping to maintain a park-like environment of the resorts while still providing enough accommodation units to make the resorts economically feasible. Urban hotels are usually higher density.

- **Building height controls** are also important in conveying the character of development and integrating it into the natural environment. In many resorts, for example, the maximum height of buildings is established at four stories (about 15 meters) so that they are below the tops of large trees and visually integrated into the environment.

- **Adequate building setbacks** from site boundaries, main roads and the shoreline are necessary to maintain open space and landscaping around buildings and give them privacy. Setbacks from the beach and shoreline are particularly important in order to retain the natural appearance of the shoreline, allow sufficient space for recreation use of the beach and public access to and along the shoreline, and prevent damage to buildings if there is erosion of the shoreline or storm flooding of the shore. In beach resorts, a setback of major buildings from the shoreline (average high tide line) of 50 meters is common.

- **Maximum floor area ratio and site coverage** standards also help to maintain the desired character of development. Floor area ratio refers to the ratio between the total floor area of the building including all storeys and the total site area. Site coverage is the percentage of the site that is covered by buildings. A maximum site coverage of 20-25 per cent is considered appropriate for good quality medium density resorts because this allows ample space for recreation facilities, landscaping and conservation areas.

- **Adequate off-street parking** must be provided for the expected number of vehicles generated by both employees and guests. Parking should usually include some large spaces for tour buses.

- **Public access** to the beach and coastline and other important environmental areas should be required so that residents can enjoy their own amenity features. However, reasonable control of access must be maintained to ensure public safety and prevent the harassment of tourists by beach vendors.

- **Sign controls** in resorts and tourism areas should be established and enforced. Large, unattractive and inappropriately located advertising signs can greatly detract from the appearance of tourism areas except for certain urban areas. Sign controls need to be established with respect to their type, location, size, materials used and night lighting. Often the approach used is not to allow any outdoor advertising signs in tourism areas, but only well-designed identification and directional signs.

- **Undergrounding utility lines** (electric power and telephone) can greatly enhance the appearance of tourism areas by precluding the need for ugly overhead utility lines. The initial cost of undergrounding is higher than installing overhead lines but maintenance costs are lower, especially in areas subject to high winds.

Architectural design

of tourist facilities establishes the character of the immediate tourism environment. Design standards should be flexible to allow for the creativity of the architect but, in any situation, certain basic principles should be observed:

- Use of local traditional or historic design styles and motifs is important so that the buildings reflect the cultural environment and give guests a distinct sense of place. This is true especially of resorts and facilities in rural areas. Urban hotels often use contemporary international styles.

- Roof lines are an important design element in conveying the character of the buildings, especially when they are low and medium rise buildings.

- Use of local building materials reinforce the local architectural style and provide economic benefits to the local area which produces the materials.

- Environmental relationships are important, for example, designing open hotel lobbies for natural ventilation in tropical environments and taking advantage of views.

Design of tourist facilities, including visitor facilities at tourist attractions, should consider use of the facilities by handicapped tourists and employees. More handicapped persons, including older persons who are semi-handicapped, are travelling and many transportation facilities such as airports already incorporate design features for the handicapped. Ramps for use by wheelchairs and low-positioned water fountains should routinely be incorporated into tourist facilities. Some hotel rooms can be designed for wheelchair use. Interpretation at attractions can include devices for the sensory-impaired.

Landscaping design

also helps convey the character of the tourist facility environment and can provide an attractive and relaxing setting for the buildings and other facilities. In resorts particularly, landscaping should be generous to give the resorts a park-like character. Landscaping includes plants of all types, water features, footpaths, outdoor furniture and lighting. To the extent possible, use should be made of indigenous plant material and be designed for low maintenance. Landscaping also provides several important functional benefits including:

- Providing shade in sunny areas.

- Providing protection from rain and wind.

- Screening unattractive views.

- Absorbing noise.

- Introducing tourists to the local plants.

- Framing views and footpaths.

- Providing privacy to selected areas such as patios.

- Absorbing carbon dioxide and emitting oxygen, thus contributing to maintaining the climatic balance of an area.

Engineering design

of infrastructure must meet international standards to maintain safety, environmental quality, hygiene and sanitation. Especially important is providing for proper collection, treatment and disposal of sewage and solid waste in order to prevent pollution, and ensuring acceptable standards of potable water supply. Roads and other transportation facilities must be designed to meet safety standards and provide for low maintenance costs.

Engineering design of buildings

must provide for minimum standards of safety such as providing proper fire exits. As referred to previously, building engineering must take into account designing for local hazards such as high winds and earthquakes. If the local area has not adopted suitable engineering standards, international standards are available such as water quality standards established by the World Health Organisation.

Architectural and engineering design should be environmentally friendly and use new environmental technologies. These include use of solar energy for water heating in hotels, use of insulation materials where appropriate to conserve energy use, installation of low-energy lamps and low-flow shower heads and toilets, use of natural ventilation in tropical areas where possible and automatic shut-off of lights when leaving hotel rooms. In small-scale developments, such as ecotourism facilities, consideration should be given to compact and odourless biological systems for on-site sanitary waste treatment and composting food waste to eliminate trucking garbage off-site. Locally produced wind or solar energy may be able to supply energy requirements for the facilities. Educating tourists to practice conservation-oriented use of facilities is also important.

TOURIST FACILITY QUALITY STANDARDS

There is much emphasis now on providing good quality tourist facilities and services. Quality development does not necessarily imply high cost but, rather, maintaining quality standards at whatever level of spending is involved. Quality tourism results in a high level of tourist satisfaction and, at the same time, protects the environment and culture of an area. Today's tourists are becoming increasingly sophisticated and expect good quality facilities and services, bypassing destinations that do not meet their expectations. Quality must be considered for both facilities and services, even though service standards are not as precise and more difficult to measure than are physical facilities.

Tourist facility quality standards are often established at the national or regional levels but, if not, they need to be adopted at the community level. In any case, local communities are often responsible for application of the standards and monitoring quality levels as tourism is developed.

Minimum standards for hotels and other types of accommodation relate particularly to health, sanitation, comfort and safety standards. These minimum requirements are typically applied through the hotel licensing and inspection procedures. Above the minimum standards, a hotel classification system is commonly used to differentiate the various quality levels of accommodation establishments. Hotel classification systems are usually based on a one- to five-star ratings but other systems are also used. These systems serve a useful purpose in indicating to travel agents, tour operators and tourists the general quality levels of the accommodation facilities in an area as a basis for deciding which facilities to select before tourists arrive at their destination. There is typically a correlation between room rates and the star ratings of hotels.

Hotel classification systems also provide a framework to hotel investors in designing their facilities to attract the desired market groups, and an incentive to the hotel owners and managers to upgrade their facilities to higher standards if they wish to do so. They are particularly useful in newly developing tourism areas where entrepreneurs do not yet understand the importance of applying quality standards and what standards should be used. Hotel classification systems are relatively complicated to prepare and apply, but many successful models exist for various regions of the world.

Restaurants must also meet minimum health, sanitation and safety standards as part of their licensing and inspection process. In some countries, restaurants are classified according to a rating system. In other places, those restaurants meeting international standards are designated as being suitable for tourist use and are typically called tourist restaurants. This designation can be especially important where there is concern about the hygienic and sanitation standards in local restaurants.

Tour and travel agencies should meet minimum standards of maintaining qualified staffs and being financially responsible as part of their licensing requirements. Tour guides should be properly trained and an examination and licensing procedure applied to tour guides. Tour agency quality standards should include that any tour buses, cars and other vehicles are efficient and safe, and that vehicle drivers are properly licensed. This also applies to car rental agencies. Other vehicles used by tourists such as taxis and tour boats should also meet safety standards and be operated in a safe manner.

An increasing number of countries have adopted consumer protection legislation for tourists This legislation requires that tour and travel agencies accurately describe the tours that they are selling and clearly state the tour pricing, and then actually provide the type and quality levels of tourist experiences and facilities and services promised in the tour programme. If they do not, they are liable to be sued by the tourists involved.

Questions for Discussion

PLANNING FOR TOURISM IN YOUR AREA

1. Are there any international tourism policies, plans or activities that affect your area and, if so, how do these influence your tourism planning?

2. Are there any national or regional tourism development policies and plans that affect your area and, if so, how do these influence your tourism planning?

3. Does your community have any general development plans and, if so, what effect will these have on tourism planning of your area?

4. If there is any existing tourism development such as nature, cultural and urban tourism, evaluate these with respect to how well they have been planned, developed and managed.

5. How adequate is access to your area and the local transportation system to serve tourism?

6. How adequate are other infrastructure facilities and services to serve tourism within your area?

7. Based on survey and evaluation of tourism resources, what types of tourism would be appropriate for your area?

8. Based on the development objectives and attractions of your area, what types of tourist markets can be attracted?

9. Summarise the major opportunities and constraints for developing tourism in your area? Can you apply SWOT analysis to developing tourism in your area?

10. Are there any constraints in developing tourism in your area resulting from carrying capacity limitations of tourism development sites?

11. What types of tourism plans should be prepared for your area: area-wide, resort, urban, nature or ecotourism, historic and cultural heritage, other types?

12. Specify the most desirable tourism development objectives for your area?

13. If specific tourism projects have been developed in your area, were they planned and developed in a systematic manner and are they being managed effectively?

14. Does your area have an environmental impact assessment (EIA) procedure? If so, is it adequate to evaluate all the impacts that should be considered in planning and developing tourism projects?

15. Does your area have any development standards and design guidelines that are applicable to tourist facilities? If so, are these standards appropriate or should they be modified?

16. Does your area have any distinctive local architectural styles that could be incorporated into the design of tourist facilities to make them interesting and reflect the local environment?

Questions for Discussion

17. How would you rate the quality standards of existing tourist facilities and services in your area?

18. Does your area have a licensing procedure for hotels and other types of accommodation? For restaurants? For tour and travel agencies? If so, do you consider the licensing requirements adequate or do they need modifications for each of these types of facilities?

19. Does your area have regulations on the safety requirements for tourist vehicles? If so, do you consider these adequate or need modifications?

20. Does your area have a hotel classification system? If so, do you consider this system adequate or need modifications?

AN OVERVIEW

Formulation of tourism plans involves application of certain principles. Although planning principles will vary depending on the local situation, there are certain basic principles that commonly apply to the various types of tourism planning.

At the sub-regional or area-wide level of planning, there should be a good access point to the area, establishment of a staging area, designation of tourism development zones such as resorts, clustering of

planning principles for tourism development

SECTION

4

tourist attractions, an efficient transportation network and adequate provision of other infrastructure. Touring circuits and tourist stopovers on the circuits should be designated. Where possible, transportation and other infrastructure should be multi-purpose serving general community needs as well as tourism.

Resort planning should be done according to a systematic process that includes market analysis and product assessment, formulating resort development objectives, feasibility studies, land use planning and relationship to local communities. An economic, environmental and sociocultural impact assessment should be conducted of the proposed project. The resort site should be carefully located according to specific criteria and various planning principles applied. Based on market trends, it is especially important that resorts incorporate a variety of recreation and other facilities. Planning should give the resort a distinct character with conservation of important environmental and historic features on the site.

Urban tourism can be very important to an area and urban tourism plans should be prepared. Historic villages, towns and urban districts should be carefully planned to retain their character as attractions for tourists and provide tourist facilities. Advantage should be taken of special attraction features such as waterfront areas and viewpoints. In urban places, it is important to develop integrated tourist information centres.

Ecotourism, a form of nature tourism in which utmost consideration is given to conservation of the environment and educating visitors about nature, should be planned according to certain principles related to conservation and developing small-scale facilities. Existing communities should be integrated into ecotourism planning. There are many other forms of tourism for which local areas may have potential and various considerations must be made in their planning.

Planning tourist attractions is carried out in a systematic manner and certain principles applied. Especially important in planning natural and archaeological/historic features is conservation of the main features with grouping of visitor facilities near the main entrance, often with accommodation located outside the site. Land use zoning is a basic technique applied in planning attractions. The performing and visual arts, crafts, ceremonies, festivals and other expressions of the area's cultural heritage must also be well planned. Accurate and creative interpretation of attractions to make them educational and interesting to tourists is essential. Efficient visitor use of attractions must be organised so that visitors can enjoy the features and they do not become overcrowded or degraded.

SUB-REGIONAL AND AREA-WIDE PLANNING

Tourism plans at this level are policy and structure plans. The policy states the type and extent of tourism development that is appropriate for the area and special considerations such as environmental protection and community involvement. The structure plan shows the access to the area, primary and secondary tourist attractions, places or sites where tourist facilities will be concentrated such as resorts and urban places, and the connecting transportation network. The type and approximate amount of accommodation to be developed in each facility development area can be indicated. Tour circuits and tourist stopovers may be delineated. Important principles for area-wide planning are:

- Establishment of a good access point or gateway for tourists visiting the area. There may be more than one primary means of access.

- Establishment of a staging area at or near the access point where there is a concentration of tourist facilities and services and often some tourist attractions. This place may serve as a base for touring the area. A major town or resort often functions as the staging area.

- Clustering of tourist attractions, often with secondary attractions combined with one or more primary attractions. Clustering of attractions will induce more tourists to visit the area and encourage them to stay longer, and provides the opportunity for more efficient provision of access and other infrastructure.

- Designation of tourism development zones such as resorts where there is a concentration of tourist facilities and services. Designation of tourism zones allows for efficient provision of infrastructure, offers a variety of easily accessible facilities and activities for tourists, encourages integrated planning and application of development controls, and limits any negative impacts in certain areas. Tourism development zones should not pre-empt areas that are more important for other uses such as agriculture, seaports, industrial development and conservation of fragile ecosystems.

- Designation of an efficient and interesting transportation network linking the tourist attractions and development area. The transportation network should allow, if possible, for organising tour circuits that form loops and minimise backtracking on the same roads.

- Development of tourist stopovers on the tour circuits where there are points of tourist interest, that offer minor tourist facilities such as restaurants, snack bars, shops and toilets. Some isolated stopovers may include small-scale accommodation.

- Provision of multipurpose infrastructure that serves general community needs as well as tourism development.

The plan will include market analysis and establishing market targets, establishing carrying capacities, recommendations on institutional elements and environmental protection measures and approaches to conserving local cultural identities and bringing benefits to local communities.

RESORT PLANNING

Resorts are integrated and relatively self-contained tourist destinations that provide a variety of facilities and activities for tourists. There are many types of resorts: beach and marine, mountain, health, recreation, and resorts serving important nature, archaeological and historic sites. They can vary in size from having many hotels with a wide variety of facilities to a single large hotel with some variety of facilities or a small 'retreat' hotel in remote areas. Resort towns are existing communities which have developed a concentration of tourist facilities and activities and are related to major attractions. An important trend in resort development is the provision of a wide variety of recreational, shopping, cultural, health and other facilities. Conference and meeting facilities are often developed in resorts. Many resorts in some countries now include self-catering accommodation and vacation and retirement homes. In addition to providing their own attractions and activities, resorts often serve as a base for tourists to tour nearby areas.

Resort planning should be carried out according to a systematic approach and process as shown in **Figure 14**. If there is not a regional or area-wide plan that designates the resort site, the complete planning process should be followed. First, a market and product assessment, especially of the tourist attractions in the area, is carried out. Then the resort development objectives, type and size are determined in preliminary form; the site selected, conceptual planning and a pre-feasibility analysis is conducted.

If the results of this analysis are positive, there is a more precise determination of the facility and land use requirements and infrastructure needs; the regional relationships are analysed, including access to the site and relationships to towns and attractions in the area; then the environmental and carrying capacity analysis is prepared. There is a feedback between the carrying capacity and amount of facilities, such as number of hotel rooms, to ensure that the site capacity is not exceeded. Relationships to local communities are analysed.

Figure 14

RESORT PLANNING PROCESS

Market & Product Assessment of Area

Determination of Objectives, Type & Size of Resort, including General Environmental Assessment of Area

Resort Site Selection

Resort Concept & Prefeasability Analysis (with feedback to above steps, project terminated if determined infeasable)

Determination of Facility & land Use Requirements	Regional Relationships	Environmental & Carrying Capacity Analysis
Determination of Infrastructure Requirements	Access to Regional Integration	Community Relationships

Formulation of Regional Relationships & Resort Land Use Plan with Phasing of Development (alternative & final plans)

Specific Environmental & Social Assessment (with feedback to plan formulation)

Economic & Financial Feasability Analysis (with feedback to plan formulation)

Implementation Program

First Stage Development

Plan Refinement of Later Phases

Implementation of Later Phases

Source: Tourism Planning: An Integrated and Sustainable Development Approach, Edward Inskeep. New York: Van Nostrand Reinhold, 1991.

Based on these analyses, the detailed resort land use plan is prepared and regional and community relationships specified. A specific environmental and sociocultural impact assessment is conducted of the resort plan to ensure that no serious environmental or sociocultural problems will be generated by the resort. If there are likely to be such problems, the resort plan will need to be modified to prevent the problems. A final economic and financial analysis is carried out to make certain that the resort will be economically viable and produce an acceptable rate of return. In a medium to large-scale resort, development may take place over a long period of time and logical phasing of development should be shown on the plan. Typically, the first phase is planned in detail and later phases are more generally planned. When the later phases are ready for development, which is usually dependent on the market conditions at that time, they can be planned in detail taking into account circumstances prevailing then, such as new tourism trends or new transportation facilities, etc.

If there are existing nearby villages where resort employees can live, any improvements needed in these villages should be included in the planning programme. If there are no nearby communities, then a new community may need to be developed for resort employees and their families or, in a small resort, a housing area provided for employees. Employee communities should include, in addition to housing, community facilities and services such as schools, medical clinics and parks and recreation facilities and adequate infrastructure.

When all aspects of the resort planning are considered satisfactory, an implementation programme is prepared, development organisational structures are determined, financing is found for development and construction is commenced. Section 5 of this guide examines implementation techniques in detail including programming development of a resort. Continuous effective management of the resort is essential in order to maintain its quality and respond to changing market and product trends. There is a tendency for successful resorts to become overdeveloped because they have been successful. Overdevelopment can lead to environmental problems and decline of the resort's popularity. The best approach is to establish a maximum size for each resort based on its carrying capacity and maintaining high quality standards. When one resort in an area is fully developed, new resorts can be developed elsewhere in the area or, in some cases, existing older resorts rehabilitated and revitalised.

Proper location of the resort is important and resort sites should be selected according to logical criteria. These criteria will vary from one place to another but successful resort sites generally should have the following attributes:

- Located at or near a tourist attraction feature such as a beach, marine area, lake, ski slope, hiking or trekking area, mineral springs (for a health resort) or major archaeological or historic site. The resort development, however, should not impinge on the feature but be set away from it.

- Desirable micro-climatic conditions as related to the type of development.

- Attractive physical environment of the site and nearby area, or possibility of making the site attractive through, for example, interesting landscaping.

- Sufficient amount of available and developable land that does not have a more important economic or conservation use.

- Good existing or potential access from the tourist gateway to the region or area.

- Existing availability of, or feasibility of developing, adequate infrastructure of water supply, electric power, waste management and telecommunications.

- No serious air or water pollution of the site and compatible nearby land uses, and limited possibility of the resort development itself generating serious environmental or social problems if it is well planned.

- Availability of a nearby labour supply to work in the resort, or the possibility of encouraging in-migration of the labour needed which might require development of a new community.

There may be additional criteria depending on the local circumstances. No single site may meet all of the criteria. But the site should meet several of the criteria with the possibility that any problems with other criteria can be resolved in the process of development.

Meetings should be held with local communities and their leaders to explain the concepts of tourism and resorts so that they can express their views on the resort proposal and commence thinking about how they can participate in and benefit from the resort development. As indicated previously, the resort plan and development programme should include ways to involve the local communities.

In preparing the resort plan, the general principles to be followed should include the following:

- Plan for a variety of recreation, nature-oriented, cultural and shopping facilities and activities within the resort and in the nearby region. Resorts now commonly include meeting and conference facilities which expand their tourist markets.

- Give the resort a distinct sense of place and character. Often the resort environment should be considered like a park in which some buildings are located.

- Plan the resort environmentally and for sustainable development with application of carrying capacity analysis.

- Establish close linkages between the resort and local communities, with these communities receiving benefits from the resorts, and to the regional context.

Some more specific principles, related mostly to land use planning and design are:

- Provide for good local and regional access to the resort.

- Conserve any existing important environmental, archaeological and historic sites on or near to the site and integrate these into the resort environment and effectively interpret the sites so that they will be appreciated by visitors.

- Group resort facilities and activity areas according to their functions.

- Maintain view planes and corridors so that the resort facilities are visually related to the major attractions of the environment such as coastal, water and mountain features.

- Properly relate the major accommodation areas to the major resort features, but do not impinge on these features.

- Provide for a centrally located and conveniently accessible resort centre (in a large resort) where there is a concentration of commercial and cultural facilities.

- Provide for a convenient, interesting but not high-speed resort transportation network. Use non-polluting public transport facilities where feasible, such as battery-powered shuttle buses and carts.

- Allow for general public access for local residents to the resort features, including its beaches if any, but also maintain public safety standards. Often public parks are now included in resorts. If residents can use their amenity features, they will not resent tourism and support its development.

- Plan for adequate infrastructure of hygienic water supply, electric power, waste management and telecommunications. Proper waste management is essential to prevent pollution problems.

- Provide for adequate housing and community facilities and services, whether these are existing or new communities, for the resort employees and their families if these are not already available in the area.

- Establish and apply suitable development standards for the resort facilities such as maximum building densities and height limits, minimum setbacks of buildings especially from the coastline, and adequate amounts of areas for landscaping and conservation features.

- Ensure appropriate architectural design of hotels and other facilities, generous and attractive landscaping and proper engineering standards of buildings and infrastructure.

- Plan the areas adjacent and near to the resort to ensure that they will be compatible with and complement the resort, and do not develop in an uncontrolled manner. It is often desirable to establish a green space zone around the resort.

- Provide for the safety of tourists, for example, providing life guards in beach resorts, ski and trail patrols in mountain resorts, ensuring that boats and other tourist vehicles meet safety standards, and incorporating basic medical emergency services in the resort development. For isolated resorts, it may be important to provide for emergency medical evacuation services.

As indicated above, provision of adequate infrastructure for the resort is essential to prevent environmental problems. Often this infrastructure can also be developed to serve nearby communities as one of the local benefits from the resort development. Conservation-oriented infrastructure techniques should be applied, such as treatment and recycling of sewage effluent for use in landscape and golf course irrigation, use of solar energy for water heating and other purposes, and use of natural ventilation in tropical areas to, in some cases, preclude the need for air conditioning. In coastal areas that have limited availability of fresh water, techniques such as reverse osmosis can be applied to desalinate salty water in order to provide adequate fresh water supplies for the resort.

URBAN TOURISM PLANNING

Tourism can be a very important socio-economic activity in cities and towns. Urban places often serve as gateways to and staging areas for tourism regions and areas or major attractions such as nature parks and archaeological sites, with tourists using the urban place as a base for regional tours and staying for some time before proceeding on. Many cities and towns have their own major attractions of museums, parks, theatres, historic districts, interesting architectural styles, shopping, restaurants, entertainment and the overall urban ambience of dynamic and bustling activities. Some urban places are important business, government and educational centres that attract business travellers and offer facilities for conferences and meetings.

Urban tourism can bring significant economic benefits of employment and income to residents. Also tourism can help support amenity features such as museums, theatres and restaurants which are also enjoyed by residents. Without tourism, some of these features would not be economically justified or much smaller in scale. Tourism can also play a major economic role in the physical and economic rejuvenation of older cities or districts of cities, towns and even villages if they offer existing or potential attractions for tourists.

Developing tourism in urban places may present some special problems because of competing demands for development of prime sites by hotels, offices and other uses, traffic congestion, and sometimes overuse of primary attraction features. If at all possible, the urban tourism plan should be prepared as an integral component of the comprehensive urban plan or an urban district redevelopment plan. In this way, tourism can be well integrated into the urban fabric and problems of conflicting land use minimised. But the urban tourism plan can be prepared separately if its relationship to overall development patterns is still carefully co-ordinated.

The planning procedure for developing urban tourism is the basic planning process of carrying out a pre-feasibility study and writing the terms of reference, setting objectives, conducting surveys and analyses, formulating alternative plans and systematically selecting the optimum plan, making recommendations on institutional elements and implementation and management. The market analysis must consider the attractions available, the role of the urban place as a base for tourists to tour the region and cater for business travellers as well as holiday tourists.

Inventory and evaluation of tourist attractions should consider improvements to existing features as well as developing new attractions. Often urban places have important historic buildings and districts of much potential tourist interest if they are restored and developed with tourist facilities and services. In many cases, existing museums and theatres can be improved and new ones developed. Shopping districts can be upgraded and pedestrianized to make them interesting for tourists. Zoos, aquariums and sealife parks, botanical gardens and cultural centres are often developed in larger cities. If these features are well developed or can be improved and utilise contemporary interpretative techniques they can be attractions for tourists as well as residents. Attractions which are located outside the urban area but accessible from it must also be considered in the planning because of their potential to provide the basis for local tours.

An important approach now being applied in many cities and towns with ocean, river and lake locations, is to develop waterfront tourist facilities. This is being accomplished through redevelopment of existing obsolete areas (often outdated port and warehouse facilities), opening up waterfront views and developing parks, promenades, hotels, museums, restaurants, shops and other attractions and facilities on the waterfront that attract both residents and tourists.

Development of meeting, conference and convention facilities is a very important consideration in planning urban tourism. These facilities can attract many additional tourists to the city. Pre- and post-conference tours are typically organised to other places in the country, region and local area which spreads the benefits of tourism. Conference facilities, however, are expensive to construct and conference tourism is very competitive, and so must be carefully analysed as to its feasibility in a particular city or town.

Historic towns and historic districts of cities, if well restored and interpreted, offer much potential for developing tourism based on the historic themes and architecturally interesting features. Conservation of historic buildings is also important to preserve the historic heritage of the area for residents to appreciate. Planning of historic urban places follows much of the same procedures and principles as for general tourism planning. However, planning of these places may require special considerations, especially of improving access to difficult sites, making effective use of narrow convoluted street patterns and provision of parking in order to minimise traffic congestion. Often the best approach is to control vehicular access with tourist vehicles parked outside the historic area and only walking or use of small non-polluting tour buses allowed within the area.

In historic preservation, except for isolated important buildings, the approach should be taken of preserving entire historic districts and not only individual buildings, so that the overall historic context and character are retained. Gardens and landscaping associated with the buildings should also be preserved and restored as an important element of the historic context. Some historic buildings are sufficiently important to be restored and developed as museums. Many historic buildings, however, can be used for tourist facilities such as accommodation, restaurants and shops, with the exteriors restored and interiors converted into these modern functions but maintaining the historic character. Other historic buildings may be used for residential purposes.

The approach commonly applied to ensure that preservation takes place is to legally designate the historic area as an historic preservation district. Historic district regulations require that the architecture of historic buildings cannot be modified unless expressly permitted. If some or all the buildings are privately owned, incentives such as tax relief can be applied to encourage restoration of the buildings. But the local authority may need to take a leadership role by restoring important buildings and offering technical assistance as well as incentives to the private owners. Any new buildings in the historic district are required to be designed in the historic style of the area or in a contemporary style that is compatible with the historic character. The economic benefits, especially from tourism, and increased property values usually justify the cost of preservation.

In summary, urban tourism planning principles include the following:

- Develop or improve urban type attractions and facilities such as museums, cultural facilities, conference facilities, interesting shopping areas, preservation of historic buildings and districts, evening entertainment and perhaps other features related to the area. Tourist attractions near to the city should be included in the planning to provide the basis for day tours outside the city.

- Take advantage of special environmental features such as waterfronts and historic districts for tourism development, and provide attractive parks, promenades and view points.

- Provide a wide variety of accommodation, restaurants and other tourist facilities including good tourist information services, and concentrate tourist facilities in certain areas related to major attractions for the convenience of tourists and efficiency of providing infrastructure.

- Provide a good public transportation network and encourage pedestrianization of tourism and shopping areas.

- Provide good tourist information services and guide maps. A strategically located visitor information centre for the urban area and environs should be developed and include information materials and services, exhibits, audiovisual presentations, books and souvenirs for sale, snack bar and toilets. In larger cities, in addition to the main visitor centre, tourist information booths can be set up in places where there are concentrations of tourists.

- Provide a variety of well guided bus tours of the city and environs and develop urban walking tours by providing guide maps and rest stops along the walking tour route.

- Provide a high level of public health with good sanitation and hygiene standards and adequate medical facilities and services for tourists.

- Maintain a high level of public safety standards with control of crime to the extent possible, and warn tourists not to visit high-crime areas and take reasonable safety precautions anywhere they are staying or touring.

- Improve the environmental quality of the urban area where needed, especially controlling air pollution and traffic congestion and promoting a clean environment, attractive building design, generous parks and landscaping including street trees.

Figure 15 describes the factors that should be considered in establishing a visitor information centre in a city or town. In the main city of the area, the visitor information centre can also provide information services for the entire area as well as the city.

ECOTOURISM PLANNING

Ecotourism is a form of nature tourism in which utmost consideration is given to conservation of the environment, including biological diversity, wildlife and ecological systems, with emphasis placed on educating tourists about the environment and how to conserve it. Ecotourism areas often include existing communities, especially of traditional peoples, and the ecotourism plan must consider ways to conserve local cultural traditions and identities and how to bring benefits to these local communities. Although still a minor component of overall tourism development on a global basis, ecotourism is expanding rapidly and tends to attract tourists who are respectful of the natural environment and local cultures.

Ecotourism particularly has potential for development in local areas that offer ecologically interesting natural environments which are often combined with settlements of traditional ethnic peoples. Because it normally tends to be small-scale, ecotourism can usually be developed within the scope of local resources, but technical assistance to the local community is often required to ensure proper development and management. Also, some financial assistance may be necessary to help the communities become involved in ecotourism. Some planning principles for ecotourism are:

- Apply strict conservation measures to the natural area to protect the flora, fauna and ecosystems and any existing archaeological or historic sites.

- Establish carrying capacity standards so that there is not over-development of tourist facilities or over-use of the environment by visitors.

- Develop small-scale tourist facilities in environmentally suitable locations, with locally based design, use of local building materials, energy-saving devices and proper disposal of waste material.. A visitor centre with exhibits about the site and local conservation techniques should be developed.

- Prepare and distribute ecotourism codes of conduct for tourists and tour operators, and monitor application of these codes.

- Provide well-trained tour guides who will give accurate information to tourists, educate tourists about biological diversity, conservation techniques and observe good conservation measures during tours.

- Integrate local communities into tourism development by providing them jobs and income from tourism, arrange village tours where

Figure 15

VISITOR INFORMATION CENTRES

Information centers exist to welcome visitors to the area, enhance the visitors' experience, and provide information so visitors will stay longer. The following planning list and questions will help focus on priorities and creative possibilities. Use the check-list and questions for discussions about where to begin, or to review what already exists. Most small communities are unable to provide everything suggested. Instead, identify what fits local circumstances.

BASIC INFORMATION:
- individual brochures or flyers about local attractions, material resources, activities, events, and local businesses (such as those for shopping, eating, entertainment)
- cultural and recreation calendars
- a guidebook of the region (including accommodations directory)
- maps of major roads, back country roads, bicycling routes, hiking trails, heritage walking tours
- referral .information for emergency services (health and vehicle)

OTHER HELPFUL INFORMATION AND SERVICES:
- attractions, activities, events, and calendars
- exhibits or displays about the area's heritage and natural history
- weather and road conditions
- tide tables, wildflower identification charts (or other information indigenous to the area)
- trip planning with suggestions of things to do or see (tailored to special interests)
- displays of local art, crafts, and other products
- a video about the area (with a comfortable viewing space)
- translation services

Evaluating Visitor information Center	Yes	No
Is the information center readily available to most visitors? Are directional signs obvious at the various entry points to the community? Are the signs readily understood by people unfamiliar with the area?	○	○
Is the information center accessible to the handicapped?	○	○
Are the setting and structure attractive? Is it reflective of the community's uniqueness?	○	○
Are services and information available when visitors need them? For instance, are they available on weekends? or in the evening, especially during the peak season?	○	○
When closed, are visitors referred to another nearby location for information or provided basic information in an outside static display?	○	○
Is an attitude of hospitality a critical factor in the selection and training of staff?	○	○
Does staff training include familiarization visits to the various tourism attractions and facilities in this and nearby communities so they can make recommendations?	○	○
Are promotional materials shared with other neighboring communities? Do we display their materials and do they display ours? Have we clearly identified which promotional materials are best distriuted here, which are best distributed elsewhere, and which need dual distribution?	○	○
Is there enough display space? Is it attractive? Is adequate and convenient storage available?	○	○

Source: Rural Tourism: Marketing Small Communities, Arlene Hetherington: Meta-Link, USA, 1991.

appropriate and educate tourists about the local cultures including their economic activities and how to show respect for their cultural traditions.

Figure 16 sets forth a checklist for planning facilities in natural areas in an environmentally appropriate manner that is compatible with the concept of ecotourism. Annex 5 presents a checklist for development of ecotourism facilities. Further guidelines and recommendations for ecotourism can be found in Guidelines: Development of National Parks and Protected Areas for Tourism, published by the World Tourism Organization.

PLANNING FOR OTHER FORMS OF TOURISM

Many areas offer opportunities for various special forms of tourism based on unusual or interesting local attractions. These forms of tourism can tap the rapidly expanding 'niche' types of tourist markets and attract tourists who tend to be environmentally and culturally sensitive. They typically do not require major capital investments and can bring benefits directly to local communities in rather remote areas. These special forms of tourism can be developed in the same country or region as larger-scale more conventional forms of tourism, although usually in different areas. However, specialised knowledge is required to develop and market these forms of tourism, and local authorities need to understand their development approaches before embarking on new ventures or advising communities or local businessmen on developing them.

Special interest tourism
is a broad category that refers to tourism that is based on specific interests of tourists and may include nature, cultural, historic or other types of themes offered in the local environment. There are hundreds of possible special interest themes ranging from birdwatching (now often called birding), wild orchid viewing, learning about natural medicines, learning about historic architectural styles and participating in archaeological excavations to studying local craft design and production and local forms of dance and music. Special interest tourism does not require luxury facilities and services but does need to be well organised and have detailed and accurate information available about the theme involved. Well-trained tour guides are essential for most types of special interest tourism to be successful. Having connections with special interest tour operators internationally is important for marketing purposes. If related to nature or cultural themes, there must be conservation of the resources involved; in this respect, advice must be sought from the relevant authorities or experts on these themes.

Adventure tourism
refers to activities of tourists that are physically challenging and involves some element of real or perceived danger. Adventure tourism includes such activities as 'white water' boating through river rapids, hiking and trekking, rock and mountain climbing, fishing, hunting and wildlife viewing in remote areas and scuba diving. This form of tourism does not necessarily require luxury facilities but the equipment involved must be of high

Figure 16

CHECKLIST FOR PLANNING TOURIST FACILITIES IN NATURAL AREAS

When planning for a new tourist facility or upgrading existing ones, the following questions must be answered. Use this checklist as a guide to consider all facets of sustainable development.

	YES	NO
Is this facility designed to respect the carrying capacity of the site?	O	O
Is this facility convenient for the user? (Consider accessibility, the flow of visitor.s, and actual use.)	O	O
Have safety factors been considered and accommodated'?	O	O
Does the form of this facility match its intended function'? (For instance, are viewing areas located where there is something to view.)	O	O
Is the facility. in keeping with the scale of the surroundings and the local style?	O	O
Does siting of buildings respect preservation of trees and minimize land cut and fill?	O	O
Are the buildings compatible and unobtrusive within their surroundings?	O	O
Have local buildings and landscaping materials been used where possible?	O	O
Does the facility interfere as little as possible with the natural ecosystem? (For instance, do roadways block streams or does effluent pollute natural waterways or water sources?)	O	O
Are roadways, walkways and trails unobtrusive, designed to minimize erosion, and control traffic flow'?	O	O
Have weather patterns been considered and accommodated?	O	O
Is year-round use possible?	O	O
Are improvements consistent with the overall master plan of the area and designated zones?	O	O
Are facilities located on the perimeter of natural areas when possible?	O	O
Have maintenance requirements been considered?	O	O

Source: Guidelines: Development of National Parks and proctected Areas for Tourism, WTO/UNEP Joint Technical Report Series, 1992.

quality and in good condition. Typically, expert guide services are necessary, safety factors must be strictly observed and environmental protection measures applied during the course of the adventure tour.

Village tourism

involves development of local style accommodation in or near interesting traditional villages where tourists stay, eat locally prepared meals and observe and participate in village activities. Facilities are constructed, owned and managed by the villagers who also provide meals (local cuisine) and other tourist services. The benefits from tourism are received directly by the villagers and tourists learn about local life styles and traditions, arts, crafts and economic activities. The villagers may provide guide services for tours to the nearby areas and organise dance and music performances for the tourists. Successful village tourism does not require large capital investment but does need to be carefully planned and managed. Villagers will need technical advice on starting their venture, training to manage and operate facilities and services, and small loans for development may be required. A joint marketing programme must be carried out, typically by the local authorities or regional or central government tourism offices. A reservation system may need to be maintained. It is important that a maximum level of tourism development, based on carrying capacity analysis, be established and respected in each village, in order to avoid environmental or social problems, with expansion taking place in new villages as needed.

Farm, ranch and plantation tourism (rural tourism)

is popular in Europe and being developed elsewhere. This form of tourism involves accommodation being offered in the farm, ranch or plantation (in tropical areas) house or in a separate guest house, providing meals and organising guests' activities in the observation and participation in the farming, ranching or plantation operations. Some establishments may operate camping facilities and allow fishing, hunting, hiking and horse riding on their property. Tourism may also be organised in fishing villages with tourists staying in local households and participating in the traditional fishing activities. Technical advice is usually required to establish rural tourism, hygienic, sanitation and safety standards must be met and typically a centralised reservation system is necessary. Rural tourism can also involve tourists visiting farms, ranches and plantations such as tea, rubber, spice and oil palm plantations or vineyards and wineries, on day tours to observe and learn about their operations but not staying overnight.

River and canal tourism

involves boating on local rivers and canals. It has become popular in many places and has potential for development elsewhere. Boats are operated as commercial enterprises taking on guests for short day tours or longer overnight tours. The boats make shorestops to visit interesting places and may offer onboard entertainment. Where stretches of rivers or canals are calm and protected, houseboats can be rented to tourists who operate the boats themselves and may take trips of several days or weeks. Adequate docking facilities are required where the boats are based or make stopovers. Benefits accrue both to the boat owners and operators in the places where the boats are based or make shorestops where the tourists purchase fuel and supplies.

Cruise ship and yachting tourism

on large lakes, seas and the oceans has become a major form of tourism in the Caribbean and Mediterranean areas. It is becoming popular in the Pacific Ocean area, especially to the Pacific Islands and points in Southeast Asia, and has potential for development elsewhere. Typical cruise ships are reasonably large and require adequate docking facilities (with sufficient berthing space and water depths of about 12 feet or 3.5 meters). Onshore facilities required include tour buses and guides, shops and restaurants and some attraction features. Duty-free shopping is often made available at the stopovers. Efficient organisation of shore stops including customs and immigration services is essential. Benefits to local communities accrue from sales made to the passengers on their shore stops and to the local tour operators. Small ship cruises can be organised to more remote areas and are often based on specific themes such as nature or traditional cultures. These cruises can help start developing tourism in coastal towns and villages with limited access and facilities, and bring some benefits to local communities from sales of crafts and tours to the passengers. Yachting tourism requires protected anchorages and marinas and onshore facilities for repairs, fuelling and supplies as well as shops and restaurants. A common approach now is for tourists to fly to a yachting centre, rent yachts for cruising the local waters, then fly home.

This type of tourism may require heavy investments in port or marina facilities, may have negative environmental impacts including periodic overcrowding of local facilities and amenity features if not controlled, and its net economic benefits to local communities in small islands are lower than land-based tourism. Therefore, its development potential must be carefully evaluated.

Road touring tourism

involves provision of facilities of accommodation, restaurants, service stations, shops and toilets alongside roads taken by tourists travelling by automobile. These facilities are very common in more developed countries where there is much automobile travel and starting to be constructed in developing countries as they become more prosperous and generate more automobile traffic. Road touring facilities can bring direct benefits to the local communities who own and operate the facilities. They should be strategically located along the roads where needed and should be planned as integrated complexes with controlled access and centralised parking, for the convenience of tourists and to minimise traffic congestion. Such complexes may even offer recreation and relaxation facilities and minor attraction features.

Railway touring tourism

is becoming popular in some places often based on tours on historic trains. Rail tours offer a combination of views from the moving trains and stopovers to visit places of specific interest as well as reaching a particular destination. Some rail tours that are well known are the Palace on Wheels, which tours places of architectural and historic interest in Rajasthan, India using restored historic coaches, the historic Orient Express in Central and Eastern Europe, the Trans-Siberian rail tour in Russia and various historic train tours in North America. Opportunities exist in many places for organising rail tours ranging from one day to several days or weeks.

Camping and caravan tourism

refers to development of camping facilities with or without tents being provided and caravan facilities to serve vehicles which incorporate living quarters (called recreational vehicles or RVs in some countries). These facilities bring benefits to local communities from sales of fuel, supplies and sometimes craft items. Campgrounds and caravan parks need to be located on or near touring roads, be carefully planned as integrated complexes with landscaping and have adequate infrastructure, especially water supply, waste management and electric power.

Residential tourism,

development of vacation and retirement homes, can generate benefits to the local area from purchases made locally and often from property taxes which help support community infrastructure and other facilities and services. It is now common practice to include residential units in integrated resorts. Residential tourism, if not carefully planned, may also result in some problems including overloading of the local infrastructure, loss of community identity, escalation of local land and housing prices, land use and environmental problems because of poor design and land being taken from conservation areas. Achieving successful residential tourism, especially outside of planned resorts, requires maintaining an appropriate level of development suitable to the local community, careful location, layout and design of housing areas and adequate provision of infrastructure.

'Roots' and nostalgic tourism

involving tourists visiting their ancestral home areas or places where they previously lived, worked, fought in wars or studied, can be an important type of tourist market to cultivate in some areas. Such tourists use conventional tourist facilities and services although some may stay with friends and relatives. Specialised tours with well trained tour guides may need to be organised for these forms of tourism.

Religious tourism

of pilgrimages being made to important religious sites, is a significant form of tourism for all religions of the world. Some sites may attract mostly domestic tourists, while others also attract large numbers of international tourists. At major religious sites, special facilities are often developed to accommodate large number of pilgrims. However, some pilgrims will also stay in local accommodation and use other local tourist facilities. Religious tourism can bring substantial economic benefits to local communities. Important religious sites also generate considerable congestion from the many visiting pilgrims which must be handled by the local authorities, and appropriate crowd management techniques must be applied to avoid problems. Because of the large numbers of tourists involved, maintaining public health and safety is a major factor.

Youth tourism

is encouraged in many places so that young people and students have opportunities for learning and recreation experiences through travel in both their own and foreign countries. Youth tourism requires organisation of transportation and tours and the development of special facilities of youth hostels offering inexpensive accommodation and meals. Dormitories associated with educational institutions can also be made available for youth groups during the school vacation periods. Youth tourism is developed for social reasons but even the inexpensive facilities can bring some benefits of employment and income to local communities.

Elderhostel

tourism is becoming popular and refers to organised travel of older persons to attend special educational programmes with provision of inexpensive accommodation, termed 'elderhostels', and other facilities. University dormitory facilities are often used as elderhostels during student vacation periods. Some elderhostel groups also engage in community service and environmental conservation programmes which are organised in co-operation with local authorities. In addition, the more conventional 'senior citizen' or 'third age' tourist market is already of considerable size, but it generally uses standard hotel accommodation and services.

Cultural exchange, study tours and home visit programmes

which encourage contact and mutual understanding among peoples of different cultural backgrounds, are already well developed in many places and have much opportunity for expansion in other areas. Cultural exchange programmes involve individuals or small groups of persons of common interests to visit and spend time in another country, touring local institutions and meeting local people. Cultural exchange programmes are typically organised by governments or special organisations. Related to cultural exchange programmes are study tours whereby groups of tourists with particular learning interests are organised to visit places where they can learn about the object of their interest. Study tours must be carefully arranged to achieve their objectives and have good guide services to interpret what the groups are visiting. Home visit programmes make arrangements for tourists to visit local homes and meet residents. Often there is a mutual interest between the hosts and guests such as the same profession or hobbies on which they can exchange information. Home visit programmes are usually organised by the national, regional or local tourism office.

There may be opportunities for other types of tourism in particular areas and all possibilities should be considered based on the assessment of tourism resources and the tourist markets.

PLANNING NATURAL AND HISTORIC ATTRACTIONS

Tourist attractions are what induce tourists to visit an area. Even some business travellers will make use of tourist attractions if they are available. In order to be successful, attractions must be carefully planned and managed. Especially important is imaginative interpretation of the attractions so that they are informative and interesting to visitors. The planning of most types of attraction features is now viewed as conserving and interpreting the environmental and cultural heritage of the area for the appreciation of residents as well as tourists. Planning heritage attractions such as nature parks, archaeological and historic sites and cultural traditions for tourism is a specialised discipline and must be adapted to each particular local situation, but some general approaches and principles are applicable to most features. The basic planning procedure for a nature or archaeological/historic site is as follows:

- Determination of the development and conservation objectives within the framework of the national, regional and local parks and monuments conservation and development policies.

- Environmental analysis including any special surveys that need to be made, such as of wildlife, vulnerable ecological systems (ecosystems) and the archaeological or historic monument, determination of special environmental areas and sites that need to be preserved and, in some cases, enhanced or restored.

- Establishment of visitor carrying capacities, based on assumptions of types of visitor use and efficient visitor organisation and flow patterns.

- Projection of visitor demand by type of use taking into account seasonality of use and reconciliation, if necessary, of demand with the carrying capacity analysis.

- Determination of the best type of interpretation to be developed for the feature, and types of visitor facilities to be developed and facility space requirements.

- Consideration of any nearby communities and other types of development and how they should interact with the attraction, including involvement of local communities and bringing benefits of tourism to them.

- Formulation of the attraction plan, including preparation and evaluation of alternative plans and selection of the final optimum plan, with staging of development indicated. Utmost consideration is given to applying environmental planning principles and protection measures in formulating the plan.

- Preparation of visitor use organisation and flow patterns where appropriate.

- Conducting the final environment impact analysis, including social considerations, with any modifications that are needed to be made to the plan.

- Determination of the best organisational approach to manage the attraction including any training required of persons to work at the attraction.

- Conducting an economic and financial analysis indicating the development and operational costs and projected revenues, with special consideration given to benefits generated to local communities including employment, income and development of small tourism enterprises. Identification of funding sources for development may be necessary.

- Preparation of the development programme and any other implementation procedures such as zoning that may be required.

- Implementation of the plan and other recommendations and continuous management of the attraction resource and its visitor use. Management includes monitoring use of the site to ensure that no environmental or other problems arise, and taking remedial action to correct problems if necessary.

Some tourist attractions such as nature or archaeological parks may not in themselves initially generate sufficient revenue to pay for their development and operational costs. However, they often generate sufficient tourist flows to the area so that the overall spending by tourists in commercial enterprises more than justifies the cost of developing and operating the attraction. Thus the attraction is economically justified if not financially justified. Eventually, direct revenues at the attraction, typically from visitor admission fees and often fees paid by local entrepreneurs, can pay for much if not all of the operational costs and perhaps costs associated with future expansion of facilities.

The planning technique normally applied at attraction sites is that of designating zones for different types of conservation and use. These zones may include strict preservation zones that, for a nature park, include rare and endangered species, important habitats and vulnerable ecosystems where only scientists and park staff are allowed, wilderness areas where the objective is resource conservation and visitor use is low-intensity with only limited facilities such as nature trails, and visitor facility zones that allow for development of campgrounds and picnic areas, a visitor centre and recreation facilities. The facility zones are typically located near the park entrances for the convenience of visitors and preclude the need to provide large-scale access to the interior of the park. Typically now permanent accommodation and other commercial facilities are located outside the park but relatively near to the park entrance for convenience of access to the park. Buffer zones are often designated to protect the conservation zones. Conservation of the important features should take precedence over visitor use. The conservation areas and related buffer zones should be legally designated as protected parks or reserves.

The use zones are connected with a circulation network of access points, roads, parking and walking and perhaps riding (horse, pony, etc.) trails. In popular parks, access by private vehicles into the park is now often prohibited. Private cars and buses must be parked at the park entrance and bus-type transportation, ideally of a non-polluting type, taken into the park, if the park is too large to tour by walking. Provision for access into the park by private vehicles must be evaluated for each particular situation.

The best approach for development of visitor facilities (except for accommodation which may be located in a separate area outside the park) is to concentrate the major facilities in one area as an integrated well-designed complex in the form of a visitor centre. This centre, typically located at the park entrance, should include interpretative material of exhibits, maps and brochures, hall for audio-visual and lecture presentations, relevant books and perhaps craft/souvenir items for sale, snack bar or restaurant and toilets. In addition to the exhibits explaining the park features, they should also emphasise the importance of conservation, the types of conservation measures being applied in the park and appropriate conservation-oriented use of the park by visitors. Personnel should be available to answer questions of visitors. Interpretative signs, rest stations, viewing sites and other small-scale facilities can be located at appropriate places in the park.

Beach and marine parks require special planning considerations. Conservation measures must be applied to the use of underwater environments in order to protect reefs and other sealife. Ecologically important underwater areas should be designated as marine parks or reserves with very strict use controls exercised. Major facilities at beach and marine parks should be set back from the beach area or coastline, behind the vegetation line. The main visitor facilities should be planned as an integrated complex, typically as a visitor centre. Often an approach used to control conflicting uses of the water area is zoning for different types of uses such as separate zones for swimming, boating, water skiing, board and wind surfing and diving (snorkelling and scuba diving).

As is the case with resort development, the areas outside but near the park should also be planned and zoned for appropriate uses and conservation. Otherwise, uncontrolled and unattractive development may take place which will detract from the general environmental quality of the area. There have been many problems with degradation of all types of conservation areas, even though they may be legally designated as protected areas, by illegal encroachment into the parks, killing of wildlife by poaching and defacement of archaeological and historic features including illegal removal of important artefacts. These problems and mitigating solutions are addressed in detail in Section 6 on maintaining the sustainability of tourism.

Techniques of interpretation of nature, archaeological/historic and other heritage sites must be applied in an imaginative manner to educate visitors and make the site more interesting to them. Interpretation of heritage features has become highly developed in recent years and includes such varied techniques as conventional guide services, audio-visual presentations, sound and light shows, interactive exhibits, re-enactment of historic places and events, use of viewing platforms and canopy walkways in rainforests to view wildlife, information signs along self-guided walking tours and many others. Concepts of conservation and sustainable development are now normally included in heritage interpretation. **Figure 17** states, as an example, the role and opportunities for interpretation of heritage sites adopted by the United States National Park Service. **Figure 18** outlines the techniques for communicating information about a heritage site to tourists and **Figure 19** presents a checklist for what visitors need to know about the site.

PLANNING CULTURAL ATTRACTIONS

Other cultural resources for tourism, such as the visual and performing arts, crafts, traditional dress, ceremonies, architecture and life styles, must be properly developed, interpreted and managed. These are also significant aspects of the cultural heritage of an area which should be preserved for the benefit of residents. In many places, cultural traditions are being lost because of the influences of modern development generally. Tourism can be an important vehicle for revitalising and conserving, often on a selective basis, these cultural traditions because they are attractions for tourists. When residents observe tourists appreciating their traditions, they will more likely take renewed pride in their culture and support its conservation.

Visual arts and crafts are an important attraction for tourists and can be a major source of income for residents of the tourism area including people living in village and rural areas. A distinction should be made between souvenir items and true arts and crafts, realising that both have a role in tourism development. The authenticity of local arts and crafts should be retained in terms of use of local designs, materials and craft skills. However, designs can often be modified to suit the interests of tourists. Where traditional arts and crafts have deteriorated, a programme may be needed to research the original designs, materials and skills employed, and training undertaken of artists and craftsmen to learn the traditional skills. Sales outlets may need to be organised and quality controls applied to ensure authenticity of the items. In some cases, the technique has been used of identifying the authentically produced items with a stamp, based on an inspection programme by the government or craft association, and informing tourists about this procedure so they will know whether they are purchasing authentic items.

Tourism can also provide a market for the contemporary arts of paintings and sculpture that are well developed in many places, often through university educational programmes. Contemporary arts can be sold to tourists at art galleries located independently or in hotels and at special exhibits.

A common and often successful approach for presentation and sale of arts and crafts is development of integrated craft centres or 'villages'. These centres are designed in the local traditional architectural style and contain a large number of shops, demonstrations of art and craft production, snack bars, restaurants and other tourist facilities. They may also provide venues for dance, music and drama performances. The craft centres should be located in attractive landscaped environments with adequate parking and have good access for tourists. Craft centres are also appropriately located in villages that specialise in production of particular types of crafts, which brings more benefits directly to the villages.

Traditional dance, music and drama performances are also of much interest to many tourists. An important factor in presentation of dance, music and drama is maintaining authenticity and quality of the performances, even though they may need to be abbreviated in time and content to suit tourists' interests and schedule. Special training programmes may need to be instituted to ensure that a high quality level of the performances is maintained. Small-scale traditional performances are usually best appreciated when held in their traditional village settings. When this approach is not possible, special performance stages or theatres can be developed for tourists.

Traditional ceremonies may also be very interesting to tourists. Each local area must decide whether to allow tourists to observe these ceremonies. If tourists are allowed, their visits should be carefully controlled so that the ceremonial procedures are not disrupted. Accurate information should be given to tourists on the background and description of the performances and ceremonies.

Traditional villages with their often distinctive layouts, architectural styles and village life generally are often of much interest to tourists. Tourist visits can also bring benefits to village residents. The concept of village tourism development was reviewed previously. Short visits by tourist groups to villages can also be arranged by tour operators if the villages agree to this. Such visits should be prearranged and carefully controlled so as not to disrupt village life, and a fee for each visit paid to the village by the tour operators. The revenues from these fees

Figure 17

INTERPRETATION OF HERITAGE SITES

Role of Interpretation

Sustainable park and ecotourism development, to be truly successful, needs to anticipate and manage human experience. Interpretation provides the best single tool for shaping experiences and sharing values. By providing an awareness of the environment, values are taught that are necessary for the protection of the environment. Sustainable design should seek to affect not only immediate behaviours but also the long-term beliefs and attitudes of visitors.

Interpretation is the communication path that connects visitors with the resources. Good interpretation is a bridge leading people into new and fascinating worlds. It brings new understanding, new insights, new enthusiasms, and new interests. To achieve a sustainable park or resource-related operation:

- Visitor experiences should be based on intimate and sensory involvement with actual natural and cultural resources. The local culture should be included. The experiences should be environmentally and culturally compatible and, through understanding and appreciation, should encourage the protection of those resources.

- Educational opportunities should include interpretation of the systems that sustain the development as well as programmes about natural and cultural resource values of the setting.

- Site and facility design should contribute to the understanding and interpretation of the local natural and cultural environments.

- Interpretation should make the values of sustainability apparent to visitors in all daily aspects of operation, including services, retail operations, maintenance, utilities, and waste handling. A good example should be set in all facets of operation.

Operations for Interpretation

A value-based visitor experience requires interpretation as an essential part of the planning and design process. Interpretative values cannot be successfully added to a development or operation as a last minute enhancement.

The primary interpretative resources of a site must be identified early in the planning process. There can be no substitute for a scientific knowledge of the resources involved; however, interpretative opportunities can usually be identified in the planning stages of a new development by answering the following questions:

- What is special or unusual about the site? (Consider both the natural and cultural aspects)
- What is particularly interesting, scenic, or photogenic about the site?
- What do visitors come to see?
- What is fun to do? (Answers must be resource-oriented and non-consumptive)
- What can be done on the site that is both environmentally sustainable and challenging?
- What resources provide particularly strong opportunities to demonstrate the underlying value system of sustainable development?
- What significant environmental controversies might be illustrated using local resources?
- What connections will the development have with the natural systems and/or cultural values of the area?
- What knowledge do visitors already have about the area?
- What knowledge and attitudes do neighbouring residents have about the site and its resources?
- What messages can be offered about sustainability that visitors can use in their everyday lives?

In addition, interpretation must be reinforced in all visitor experiences and inherent in management's thinking and in the relationship of the proposed development to the larger cultural context. The value system that interpretation communicates must pervade the entire cycle of the planning, design, construction, operation and maintenance.

Source: Guiding Principles of Sustainable Design by the United States Department of the Interior, National Park Service, Denver Service Center. September, 1993.

Figure 18

TECHNIQUES FOR COMMUNICATING TOURIST INFORMATION

Brochures:

These should be colourful, attractive and interesting. Some are for wide distribution, such as in tourist offices. They should lure visitors, describe what can be seen or done, explain how to get there, and identify any special preparations required such as reservations, permits, or special equipment. The brochure or leaflet can outline the costs, conditions and facilities available in and around the site or destination. Other brochures (available in several different languages if there are many international visitors) can provide visitors with basic information to help them make the most of their time when on site, including brief descriptions, a detailed map, and a list of regulations or recommendations.

Self-guided trails or tours:

Visitors can be provided brochures with maps and other information about individual displays which are marked - perhaps by a numbered post or label. Or, instead of a brochure, the information may be on sign boards along a trail or at various spots in an historical building or museum. A self-guided trail or tour can expand the tourists' understanding and appreciation of the site, allowing them to move about at their own pace, without requiring additional staff.

Guided tours:

A trained guide or docent can accompany groups of visitors, discussing features along the way. Such a tour has an advantage because the guide can adapt what is said to the particular interests of each group. The method is especially useful with school children and formal tour groups, or as a means of controlling traffic flow. In any case, guides must be knowledgeable about many aspects of the attraction, and be fluent in the major languages of visitors.

Visitor information centres:

These are special buildings or rooms in which detailed information can he displayed. Exhibits may include photographs arranged in wall or panel displays, map models, mounted specimens, or diagrams. Visitor centres are very useful for showing processes, histories and other features that cannot be seen on a short visit or understood without explanation. Where necessary, information centres can be enlarged or combined with education centres. In addition, detailed books and guides can be available for sale.

Education centres:

These are special buildings, or separate spaces within the information centre, capable of more formal educational activities or displays. They usually have facilities to hold classes or discussion sessions and are often equipped with audio-visual equipment for slide shows, films or video productions. Permanent and continuous audio-visual presentations are frequently used.

Displays and exhibits:

Displays and exhibits are useful because they are self-pacing, can be portable, and located indoors or outdoors. The most effective displays and exhibits have a clearly defined theme and have been planned with a specific audience in mind. The variety can include objects and specimens, dioramas, scale models, live exhibits, panels of text, diagrams, and photographs.

Informal contact:

As staff moves about their normal duties they can casually engage visitors in conversation, provide relevant information, and obtain some feedback. In order for the contact to be effective, however, the staff must be knowledgeable, which may require training in visitor communication and hospitality.

Source: Guidelines: Development of National Parks and Protected Areas for Tourism, WTO/UNEP Joint Technical Report Series, 1992.

Figure 19

CHECKLIST FOR WHAT VISITORS NEED TO KNOW

	YES	NO
Have you told visitors what there is to see and do, so they can plan their visit and make the best use of time in keeping with their particular interests?	○	○
Are there maps or signs showing how to get to the attraction and how to get from one place to another while there?	○	○
Have you explained what the visitor is looking at? Is the information simple, brief, basic and interesting?	○	○
Have you explained regulations, including what is and is not allowed and why? (Consider the message carefully. "Don't walk on the grass" is clear but can be offensive. "Walk on the pathways only" is better. But "Please walk on the pathway so as not to disturb The delicate wildflowers" is best of all.)	○	○
Have you communicated your purpose for being? (For instance, a wildlife preserve might explain the purpose of a protected area, the relationship of the protected area to its surroundings, and its importance in the world system of protected areas.)	○	○
Have you provided a reason for the visitor to come back again ? (For instance, you might mention noteworthy seasonal happenings such as the arrival of migratory birds or harvest activities or a local festival.)	○	○
Have you asked for visitor feedback or participation'? (This could include suggestions or complaints, donations of time or money, commitment to and requests about conservation or preservation organizations).		

Source Guidelines: Development of National Parks and Protected Areas for Tourism, WTO/UNEP Joint Technical Report Series, 1992 can be used to improve village facilities and infrastructure. The villagers can also make crafts for sale to tourists and, in some cases, prepare lunch or snacks for the tour groups. Where it is considered too disruptive to village activities to allow tourists to visit the local villages, a model village can be established to demonstrate to tourists the village layouts and architecture and typical village activities. These model villages function as outdoor museums with guides and descriptive material available.

Efforts should be made to introduce tourists to the local cuisine which is an important expression of the cultural heritage of an area. Local cuisine also utilises locally produced food items and local knowledge and skills in cooking techniques. The cuisine should be well explained to tourists so that they know the types of ingredients and preparation techniques used. In some cases, the local dishes may need to be somewhat modified to be acceptable to tourists' tastes but should still retain their unique character.

An approach to encourage more interest by both residents and tourists in the local visual and performing arts, crafts, traditional dress and cuisine, and in improving the quality and authenticity of these, is to organise annual arts or cultural festivals. These festivals can attract performing groups, artists and craftsmen from throughout the area. Awards can be given to the best in each category which provide incentives for high quality presentations. These festivals often start as being primarily for the enjoyment and benefit of local residents and, as they become more professional, attract domestic and foreign tourists. Some festivals, such as the Carnivals in Rio de Janeiro, Venice or Trinidad and Mardi Gras in New Orleans are major attractions for both domestic and international tourists. Sometimes, festivals can be scheduled during the typical low tourist season in order to attract more tourists during that period.

It is common practice to consolidate cultural activities of an area in a cultural centre that offers a combination of facilities: one or more performing stages, exhibit areas, perhaps a museum, meeting rooms, a snack bar or restaurant and other visitor facilities. In addition to routine use, special arts or cultural festivals can also be held in the centres.

PLANNING SPECIAL TYPES OF ATTRACTIONS

Various special types of attractions and related facilities can be considered by local authorities to supplement the primary natural and cultural attractions. Planning for these special attractions are reviewed in the following sections.

Theme parks

man-made attractions based on particular themes such as cultural patterns and historic periods, the natural environment, future technology and adventure and often a combination of themes, are currently very popular. Some basic considerations in planning theme parks include:

- Base the theme of the park at least in part on local cultural, historic or environmental subjects that will reinforce the unique character of the area and present something unusual to the visitors.

- Prepare a careful feasibility study to determine market, financial and economic feasibility—good quality theme parks are expensive to build and operate and not all theme parks are successful.

- Select the site carefully so that it has good regional access and can serve a broad market.

- Provide good local access and other infrastructure.

- In addition to planning the theme park itself, plan the area around the park and integrate it into area-wide development planning.

- Provide good management and maintenance including maintaining a clean, safe and hygienic environment.

- Be prepared to update and revitalise the theme park periodically so that it does not lose its markets.

Gambling casinos or gaming tourism

have been developed in some places as a primary or secondary attraction. Entertainment is often associated with gambling casinos. In developing gaming tourism, consideration must be given to the social impact on the local communities and possible association with prostitution, organised crime and drugs. In places where local incomes are low or in societies where gambling is a compulsive activity with some people or where there are moral or religious opposition to gambling, a consideration is whether to allow local residents to gamble. In many places, sufficient attractions can be developed without introducing gambling, at least as a major activity. Each area must decide whether to consider developing gaming tourism and, if so, under what circumstances.

Shopping

is an important attraction for many tourists and can be a significant source of income for the tourism areas. Shopping relative to arts and crafts has already been reviewed. Shopping for speciality items such as fashion designer clothing and jewellery can be an attraction in places that offer these designer resources and materials. Speciality shopping requires well located and attractively styled shops that convey an exclusive character. Traditional markets and bazaars are important attractions in many places, but these must be accessible to tourists, be well maintained and provide a clean and safe environment if many tourists are to visit them. If prices are typically cheaper than in the tourists' home countries, shopping for general goods may be an attraction if proper shopping facilities are available. 'Duty-free' shopping for goods that are partially or fully exempt from import duties, has been well developed in some countries, especially at airports. Successful duty-free shopping requires careful market analysis and pricing and attractive, clean user-friendly shopping facilities. Analysis, design and development of duty-free shopping facilities is a specialised area of tourism planning.

Conference

convention and meeting facilities, especially in cities and large resorts, can attract large numbers of tourists who use local tourist facilities and services and often also visit local attractions. Although not attractions in themselves, these facilities should be considered in planning the local tourism area. Development of conference and convention tourism requires several considerations:

- Prepare a thorough market, financial and economic feasibility analysis—conference and convention tourism is very competitive.

- For large-scale convention facilities, locate them in a city or resort that has good international, national and regional access.

- A large undeveloped site, or a site that can be redeveloped, including sufficient land for parking must be available. A convention centre can be used as a technique to achieve redevelopment of blighted urban area.

- The conference centre should be in a central location and accessible to good quality hotels and local transportation. Often a conference centre will be physically associated with a large good quality hotel, and even be operated by the hotel. The hotel can provide the banqueting services needed in a large conference centre.

- The conference centre should be close to major shopping, entertainment and recreation facilities for use by persons attending the conference in their spare time.

- Interesting attractions in the local area or region should be available for tours by conference participants. Often pre- and post-conference tours are organised in the region for participants.

- Experience in organising conferences is essential. Conference organisation can be contracted to a competent firm or handled by a nearby hotel.

- Smaller-scale meeting and conference facilities should be routinely incorporated in hotels and resorts. Smaller conferences, meetings, seminars and workshops can be an important type of business for hotels or resorts. Some large resorts may have major conference facilities.

Evening entertainment

is important to consider in planning a tourism area, especially in urban and resorts tourism. Many tourists visiting these places wish to engage in some evening activities and become bored if they are not available. Evening entertainment can range from traditional performances and conventional theatre to night clubs and discos. Even providing an evening video movie or lecture on the local environment and culture in a resort hotel can be entertaining for some guests.

Facilities for major sports events and fairs/expositions

require large sites, excellent accessibility both to the general area and the facilities complex, integrated planning of the facilities, and availability of accommodation, restaurants and other tourist facilities. Excellent organisational capabilities are essential for the success of large-scale events. Even though they might be developed for a single upcoming event such as Olympics or international exposition, planning for the facilities should consider long-term permanent use which will bring lasting benefits to the area.

PLANNING FOR VISITOR USE OF ATTRACTIONS

In addition to physical planning and conservation of tourist attractions, visitor use of the sites must be carefully programmed so that the attraction serves its intended purpose of serving satisfied visitors without it becoming degraded. Basic considerations for planning efficient visitor use of attractions are:

- Providing for visitors to have ample opportunity to enjoy, appreciate and understand the attraction feature. The importance of effective interpretation of the site has already been emphasised.

- Ensuring that the carrying capacity of the site is not exceeded so that the site is not degraded and a high level of visitor satisfaction is maintained.

- Ensuring that visitor use does not degrade the site or result in environmental problems.

- Ensuring that residents of the area also have the opportunity to visit the feature at affordable cost.

- Various techniques to avoid overuse of a particular site include:

- Decentralisation of tourism to various attractions in the area to take the pressure off any one site.

- Prepare and apply a logical visitor flow plan for tours of the site.

- If the site is particularly vulnerable to excessive visitor use, develop a model of the feature that tourists can visit and only allow scientific use of the original feature.

- If queuing of visitors is necessary, make it interesting with simple entertainment so that visitors do not become bored and irritated while they wait.

- Apply techniques to reduce seasonality of tourism because the high demand period is often when a site is subject to overuse and degradation. Seasonality considerations are examined in Section 7 on managing tourism.

Attraction sites should be continuously monitored so that any problems can be detected in their early stages and remedial action taken. It is more difficult to correct problems after they become serious. Special surveys of visitors should periodically be conducted to determine their satisfaction levels, any complaints they have and how they believe the site and its interpretation could be improved.

PREPARING TOURISM PLANS IN YOUR AREA

1. What do you think would be the most appropriate tourism development policy for your area with respect to: Type and extent of tourism development? Developing tourism? Developing domestic tourism? Environmental protection? Community involvement? Other factors?

2. How would you apply the basic planning principles to area-wide planning in your area, such as entry point and staging area and designating tourism development zones?

3. Are there opportunities for developing touring circuits and tourist stopovers in your area?

4. Is there potential for developing resorts in your area? If so what would be suitable types of resorts?

5. If there is potential for development of resorts in your area, can you select logical sites for resort development based on the site selection criteria?

6. Based on a selected resort site in your area, can you apply the resort planning principles to prepare an integrated resort development plan?

7. If there is potential for developing urban tourism in your area, what types of improvements, including tourist attractions and facilities, in the city are required to make urban tourism successful?

8. If there is potential for developing ecotourism in your area, what approach and principles would you apply to ensure conservation of the site and generating benefits to local villages?

9. What are all the types of special interest and adventure tourism that you believe would have potential for development in your area? What approaches would you use in their development?

10. What other specialised forms of tourism can be developed in your area, and what would be the most suitable approach in developing these: village, rural, river and canal, cruise ship, yachting, road touring, railway touring, camping, residential, roots and nostalgic, religious, youth, etc.?

11. If there are potential natural attractions in your area, what recommendations would you make to develop them for visitor use, applying the planning principles set forth in this section? If these features already attract some visitors, how could visitor facilities be improved?

12. If there are archaeological or historic sites in your area, what recommendations would you make to develop them for visitor use, applying the principles set forth in this section? If these features already attract some visitors, how could visitor facilities be improved?

13. What types of interpretation techniques would be the most suitable for the tourist attractions in your area? Natural attractions? Archaeological/historic attractions? Other types?

Questions for Discussion

14. If your area has existing or potential production of crafts, what would be the best programme for improving and expanding craft production and providing sales outlets? Would it be appropriate to develop a craft centre in your area?

15. If your area has performing arts of dance, music, drama, etc., how can these best be presented to tourists?

16. How can shopping facilities and services including types of shopping be improved for tourists in your area?

17. Is there need for development or expansion of conference and meeting facilities in your area?

18. Would gaming tourism (gambling casinos) be appropriate to develop in your area?

19. Would theme parks be suitable and feasible to develop in your area? If so, what type of theme park would be most appropriate?

20. If there are existing attractions in your area, how well is visitor use organised at these places? How could visitor use be improved?

AN OVERVIEW

Implementation of tourism policies and plans is the responsibility of both the government and private sectors. The public sector is responsible for policy, planning and research; providing basic infrastructure; developing some tourist attractions; setting and administering facility and service standards; establishing and administering land use and environmental protection regulations; setting standards for and

implementing tourism development

encouraging education and training for tourism; maintaining public safety and health; and some marketing functions. The private sector is responsible for developing accommodation, tour and travel operations and other commercial tourism enterprises and related on-site infrastructure, some tourist attractions, and some marketing activities. In newly developing tourism areas, the government must often assume a strong role in facilitating and co-ordinating tourism development. Political commitment to developing tourism in a planned and sustainable manner is essential. Increasingly, non-government organisations (NGOs) are involved in aspects of tourism development.

Various implementation techniques should be applied. Logical staging and programming of development projects and other actions required (the tourism action programme) is essential. There must be effective organisation of the public and private sectors in tourism. Appropriate legislation must be applied for tourism including land use and environmental protection regulations and tourist facility standards. Specific tourism projects should be developed in a systematic manner applying critical path analysis techniques. Securing financing for both public and private sector tourism projects is a crucial activity in implementation, and all possibilities should be considered. Each area should devise a strategy for financing tourism development. Communities must be involved in tourism development and several techniques can be used to encourage community participation in tourism in their areas.

Human resource development for tourism must be given priority in order to offer the quality of services expected by the tourist markets. Developing the human resources for tourism requires a systematic approach of projecting personnel needs and determining the training required to provide the qualified personnel. Personnel in both the public and private sectors require education and training. There are several training approaches which should be considered. If national and regional hotel, catering and tourism training institutions cannot satisfy local needs, then a training institute may need to be established locally.

Effective marketing of tourism in the local area is essential . Marketing objectives and strategies must be determined and a promotion programme carried out. There are several types of promotion techniques which can be used. Marketing activities must be co-ordinated among the various levels of government tourism offices and between the local tourism office and private tourism sector. Developing a desirable image of a new tourism area in the potential tourist markets is very important. Marketing includes providing tourist information services in the local area.

RESPECTIVE ROLES OF THE PUBLIC AND PRIVATE SECTORS

Implementation of tourism policies and plans requires various approaches and techniques. As previously emphasised, planning recommendations should be made that are capable of being implemented and ways to accomplish implementation should be considered throughout the planning process. Implementation is the responsibility of both the government and private sector, and the respective roles of the public and private sectors need to be clearly defined in the implementation process. The present policy of most countries is that the private sector is now expected to play the lead role in all types of development including tourism. However, in newly developing tourism areas where private sector capabilities are still limited, the government must still play a strong role in co-ordinating development and managing the tourism sector. Government should be viewed as the facilitator of development. Also, community understanding and support of the plan are essential.

Public sector roles in developing tourism are typically policy, planning and research; providing basic infrastructure; developing some tourist attractions; setting and administering tourist facility and service standards; establishing and administering land use and environmental protection regulations; setting standards for and encouraging education and training for tourism; maintaining public safety and health; and some marketing functions. Offering incentives to attract private sector investment or even joint venturing with the private sector on some projects may also be necessary to encourage private initiative in development. Political commitment to developing tourism in a planned and sustainable manner is essential to provide the foundation for implementation. Achieving this commitment often requires educating policymakers about the potential importance of tourism in the area and the need to develop it according to sustainable principles.

The private sector is generally responsible for developing accommodation, tour and travel operations and other commercial tourism enterprises and related on-site infrastructure, some tourist attractions and some marketing activities. The private sector should also assume some self-regulatory functions in maintaining industry quality standards through private sector tourism associations. Much of the infrastructure can be provided by private utility companies or public corporations, with user fees paying for the investment and operational costs involved.

Maintaining close co-operation and co-ordination between the public and private sectors throughout the planning and implementation process is essential, so that development is co-ordinated and directed toward achieving common objectives. A common organisational mechanism is to establish a co-ordinating body on tourism in the area, such as a tourism advisory board or co-ordinating committee comprised of representatives of government and the private sector. This body meets regularly to consider tourism matters of mutual interest, exchange ideas and information, advise responsible authorities to take appropriate actions and co-ordinate joint sponsorship of some projects. In addition, there needs to be informal contacts between government authorities and the private enterprises on a continuous basis.

Increasingly, non-governmental organisations (NGOs) are involved in aspects of tourism such as conservation of natural, historic and cultural resources that tourism can use, developing ecotourism and community-based projects and improving craft production and sales. NGOs can often perform a valuable role in developing tourism, especially at the village and rural levels. Close co-ordination should be maintained with involved NGOs and their participation in tourism encouraged where it is appropriate.

IMPLEMENTATION TECHNIQUES

Implementation of tourism plans involves various approaches and actions being carried out over a long period of time. Basic approaches to implementation are:

- Legal adoption of the tourism policy and plan as the official guide for tourism development in the area.

- Logical staging of development, usually by five-year periods, and programming of development projects and other actions required (usually called the tourism action programme) for the first five-year period of implementation.

- Effective organisation of the public and private sectors in tourism and close co-ordination maintained between the public and private sectors and with NGOs where they are involved. Organisational structures are examined in Section 7.

- Adoption and application of appropriate legislation and regulations for tourism development. These include regulations on tourist facility and service standards, land use (zoning) and environmental protection regulations, and development standards (usually included in the land use zoning regulations) and design guidelines for tourist facilities.

- Effective tour programming of routes and stopovers for sightseeing tourists.

- Efficient implementation of individual tourism projects according to a systematic approach.

- Adequate financing of public sector tourism functions including development of tourist attractions and infrastructure. In some places, outside assistance may be needed on this financing.

- Attracting private sector investment in the development of tourist facilities and services. Investment incentives may be required to attract this investment.

- Proper education and training of persons to work in all aspects of tourism—this is human resource development (HRD) for tourism.

- Involving local communities in tourism development.

- Effective marketing and promotion of tourism for the entire area and for individual enterprises.

- Effective continuous management of the tourism sector, as is described in Section 7.

Development programming

is an important technique to achieve systematic and co-ordinated implementation. Often this takes the form of an action programme which includes both development projects and other actions required. The action programme for the first stage of development, usually the first five-year period of the plan, is often prepared as part of the initial tourism planning process, and is then updated and revised periodically. The action programme should include both public and private sector projects and infrastructure as well as attractions, facilities and services required so that development is integrated and co-ordinated. Other actions needed might be, for example, drafting and adopting certain types of regulations. The programme may include special studies or detailed planning that should be carried out during the five-year period. **Figure 20** presents a model tourism development action programme for expansion of a tourism area, which can be used as a guide. A complete action programme would describe each project, indicate development cost estimates where appropriate and designate the responsible agency for carrying out the project.

Zoning

is an important technique to ensure implementation of land use plans for resorts, tourist facilities at attraction sites, tourism in cities and towns and other types of local tourism areas. As referred to previously, zoning regulations typically include development standards such as densities, height limits and setbacks although these can also be adopted separately for tourism areas. Zoning should also be applied to control development near tourism areas so that it is compatible with tourism. Zoning is used for all types of land uses, not only tourism, and zoning regulations may already

Figure 20

MODEL TOURISM DEVELOPMENT ACTION PROGRAMME

Tourist Facilities

PROJECT/ACTION	Year 1	Year 2	Year 3	Year 4	Year 5
Urban hotel expansion	Planning & design	Construct	Open		
New urban hotel	Planning & design	Construct	Construct	Open	
Beach hotel 1	Planning & design	Construct	Construct	Open	
Beach hotel 2		Planning & design	Construct	Construct	Open
Mountain lodge			Planning & design	Construct	Open
Tour agency 1	Organize	Open			
Tour agency 2				Organize	Open
Tour stopover & restaurant 1	Planning & design	Construct	Open		
Tour stopover & restaurant 2			Planning & design	Construct	Open
Tourist information center	Planning & design	Construct	Open		
Restaurant & craft shops			Open	Open	Open

Tourist Attractions

National Park		Overall Planning	Facilities design	Construct facilities	Open
Beach-Marine Park	Planning & design	Construct facilities	Open		Expand facilities
Historic site 1	Planning	Restoration	Construct facilities	Open	
Historic site 2		Planning	Restoration	Construct facilities	Open
Cultural center	Planning	Construct design	Construct	Open	
Museum expansion	Design	Construct	Open		

Infrastructure

Airport expansion	Planning	Construct	Construct	Open	
Beach area roads	Planning	Construct	Construct	Open	
Beach area water & electricity supply	Planning	Construct	Construct	Open	
Expansion of sanitation and solid waste disposal	Planning	Develop	Expand		
Mountain roads		Planning	Construct	Construct	Open
Mountain area water & electricity supply			Planning	Construct	Open

Other Projects & Actions

Tourism law & regulations	Review adopt				
Investment incentives	Review adopt				
Tourism office & tourism promotion board	Establish	Initial staff training		Expand	
Tourism awareness programme	Organize	Commence	Continue	Continue	

be adopted for the tourism area and tourism zones can be added to these. If not already existing, environmental protection legislation and the environmental assessment procedure will need to be adopted to protect the overall environment. The basic building code or regulations including the fire code for the area should be reviewed to make certain that they meet good standards for tourist facilities.

Administration of site planning, architectural and landscaping design guidelines

for tourism areas such as resorts and historic districts is often done by an architectural review board or committee which is established for this purpose. This body must review, and require modification if necessary, all proposed tourism development projects with respect to meeting design standards which have been set by the board. As mentioned previously, the architect and other designers of the development should have considerable flexibility to exercise their skills and creativity. The design review board procedure, however, ensures that the design is compatible with the intended physical character of the facilities, and is harmonious with the area's local environmental conditions and architectural traditions.

Other regulations

must also be prepared and adopted relative to tourist facility and service quality standards, especially related to health, safety and sanitation. These regulations include licensing requirements and inspection procedures of hotels and other types of accommodation, restaurants, tours and travel agencies and tour guides. A hotel classification system may need to be prepared and adopted. Other necessary regulations such as safety factors on tourist vehicles and boats may need to be prepared and adopted. Engineering standards for infrastructure and building codes should be reviewed to make certain that they meet acceptable standards.

Tour programming

is based on the plan's recommendations for development of tourist attractions and the transportation network. In addition to providing an important activity for tourists, well-designed and imaginative tour programmes can benefit an area by spreading economic benefits more widely geographically and throughout society. Development of tourist facilities and services such as restaurants and craft shops along the tour routes encourage tourist spending at those stopovers. The tourist markets can be broadened and the length of tourists extended through offering a variety of interesting tours and new tourist experiences.

Tour programmes may include, in addition to the traditional bus and taxi tours, walking and horse (or other animal) riding tours, boat tours on lakes, rivers, canals, bays and harbours and railway tours. River tours may, for example, provide the opportunity for tourists to visit remote villages which are not otherwise accessible, thus bringing some benefits to those places. Local air tours, by aeroplane or helicopter, are popular in some areas although these can generate considerable noise pollution.

Project development

can be a complicated process, especially for large projects such as resorts with several hotels and a variety of other facilities. Careful development programming is required utilising critical path analysis. This is a technique for scheduling actions to be carried out in the most logical and efficient sequence to implement a project in a co-ordinated manner. It is usually shown in a diagrammatic format. **Figure 21** presents a model development programme for a resort complex. An actual development programme would be more detailed. Projects seldom exactly follow their pre-arranged schedules, and adjustments must be made as the project proceeds. However, without a critical path programme, implementation would be much less efficient and there would not be a framework for monitoring the work activities and keeping them on track.

Commercial projects are usually undertaken by the private sector. Major projects such as resorts require substantial initial investment, especially for the infrastructure, and it may be several years before revenues are generated from the commercial activities. Such projects also require considerable managerial experience to succeed. If the local private sector is weak and lacks managerial experience or sufficient capital to develop major projects, a public development corporation may need to be established. A public development corporation is funded by the government or jointly by the government and private sector, can borrow money and is capable of employing experienced managers. The corporation is responsible for developing the infrastructure, landscaping and other non-commercial components of the project, and may continue to manage these components after the resort operations are underway. The corporation typically leases the commercial sites, such as hotel sites, to the private sector for development, with the revenues from the leases used to repay the capital investment costs and support the operational expenses of the resort. The development corporation may also be structured to develop more than one tourism project in an area.

FINANCING TOURISM DEVELOPMENT

Adequate financial resources are essential for developing tourism. Several types of financing are required:

Funding for tourism planning and management.

Financing general tourism planning at the local level, such as area-wide, urban and ecotourism plans, and planning for public-type attraction features, such as national parks and archaeological/historic sites, is typically the responsibility of the government. Financing more detailed planning of development sites and project feasibility studies is usually the responsibility of the private sector. Planning of a large resort may be either by the government, private company or development corporation. Even though the planning is done by the private sector, government has the responsibility to set the standards as has been previously described, review the plans and approve them only if they meet acceptable standards. Financing the government tourism office and general destination marketing is by the government, but this funding can be supported, in part, by a hotel or tourist expenditure tax, or for marketing, by joint promotion boards with contributions from both the public and private sectors.

Figure 21

MODEL RESORT DEVELOPMENT PROGRAMME

ACTIVITY	YEAR 1	YEAR 2	YEAR3	YEAR 4	YEAR 5
Resort Planning					
Preliminary land use plan					
Public review					
Feasibility analysis					
Final land use plan					
Infrasructure plan					
EIA					
Public review					
Infrastructure Development					
Final design					
Off-site improvements					
On- site improvements					
Roads					
Water and energy supply					
Sewage disposal					
Irrigation system					
Telecommunications					
Solid waste disposal and sanitation					
General landscaping					
Final design					
Project nursery					
Installation & maintenance					
Golf Course					
Design of fairways					
Design of club house					
Development-stage I					
Development-stage 2 (after 5 years)					
Accommodation					
Hotel I					
Design					
Public review					
Construction					
Hotel 2					
Design					
Public review					
Construction					
Hotel 3					
Design					
Public review					
Construction					
Other hotels after 5 years					
Condominiums					
Design					
Public review					
Construction-stage I					

MODEL RESORT DEVELOPMENT PROGRAMME Continued)

ACTIVITY	YEAR 1	YEAR 2	YEAR3	YEAR 4	YEAR 5
Construction-stage 2 (after 5 years)					
Other Facilities					
Resort center					
Design		▬			
Public review		▬			
Construction-stage 1			▬▬▬▬▬		
Construction-stage 2 (after 5 years)					
Beach park					
Design			▬		
Public review			▬		
Development			▬▬▬▬		
Historic Site					
Design			▬		
Public review			▬		
Restoration			▬▬▬▬		
Tennis complex					
Design			▬		
Construction			▬▬▬		
Boat jetty					
Design			▬		
Construction				▬▬	
Employee Housing					
Land use & Infrastructure plan		▬▬			
Public review		▬			
Housing design			▬▬		
Public review			▬		
Construction stage-1			▬▬▬		▬
Construction stage-2 (after 5 years)					
RESORT OPENING				▬	

Note: This simplified development programme assumed that the site has already been selected, the prefeasability analysis conducted, and the land acquired, or that the developer has an option for purchase of the land. This option usually depends on public review of the preliminary land use plan. Acquisition occurs during the first year of the programme.
The design phase, which is indicated for the facility components, includes site planning and design of on-site infrastructure, buildings, and landscaping.

Construction includes site preparation, on-site infrastructure and landscaping development, and construction of buildings. As indicated, this programme is for the first stage of development, followed during the next five-year period by a second stage. Typically, temporary infrastructure is developed to commence construction of facilities so that final infrastructure does not need to be complete before facility construction starts. This scheduling does not allow for the additional time often required for negotiations with hotel developers. It also assumes a rapid public review process, which, in fact, often requires more time, especially to prepare revisions made in response to the public review

Source: Tourism Planning: An Integrated and Sustainable Development Approach Edward Inskeep. New York: Van Nostrand Reinhold 1991.

Funding of infrastructure development.

Major types of infrastructure are typically financed by the government or utility companies. However, user fees can recover much of this investment or at least the operational costs. This infrastructure also serves general development needs. Financing of on-site infrastructure for development projects is usually by the private sector party that is undertaking the development.

Funding of major attraction features.

National, regional and local parks, archaeological and historic sites, museums, cultural centres and some other types of attractions are normally financed by the government, but with admission fees paying for at least the operational costs. These attractions are what induce tourists to visit an area and spend money in commercial enterprises, and they serve residents as well as tourists. Therefore, they should not be expected to be totally self-financing. As explained previously, financing restoration of historic districts can be provided by the private sector but often with government offering incentives. Commercial-type attractions, such as theme parks, are financed by the private sector and expected to produce profits.

Funding of hotels and other commercial facilities and services.

The private sector is the normal source of finance for the development of hotels and other commercial facilities and this is the policy and trend in most areas. Promotion of individual enterprises is financed by the owners/managers of the enterprises. However, as previously mentioned, the government may need to be a pioneer developer in new tourism areas until private investors have the confidence to make investments, or government establishing joint ventures with private investors for specific projects.

Investment incentives are often needed, at least in the initial stage of development, to attract private sector investors in tourism. Investment incentives may already be adopted at the national or regional levels. These may be adequate or the local area may wish to consider offering additional incentives. Where there are no incentives offered at the national or regional levels, the local authorities may wish to take initiative in providing incentives. Types of incentives which can be considered include the following:

- Provision of land at moderate or no cost for development of tourist facilities at suitable sites. In some areas where land acquisition by the private sector is difficult, just the assembly of land by the government is sufficient incentive.

- Provision of off-site infrastructure at no cost to the developer. In any case, this is commonly provided.

- Provision of all or part of the on-site infrastructure for which the cost may eventually be recovered through user fees or lease rent of the hotel and other commercial sites.

- Complete or partial exemption from customs duties on imported items used in the initial development and perhaps operation of the tourist facilities. This is offered by the national government, not the local authorities.

- Complete or partial exemption from company income taxes on profits made for a specified period of time, that is, a tax holiday. This is typically offered by the national or regional government.

- Complete or partial exemption from property taxes at the local level for a specified number of years.

- Provision of development loans at regular or low rates of interest, or guarantee by government of loans made by private institutions. Allowance can be made for extended period of grace on repayment of loans.

- Provision of grants for development up to a certain percentage of investment cost, or grants for staff training programmes.

Other types of incentives may be appropriate in certain circumstances. Where government and private capital resources are limited for developing tourism., international assistance can be sought. Interna-tional sources of funding for technical assistance on tourism planning, training and related activities and for actual development include the following:

- The World Bank Group including the International Finance Corporation, which finances private sector commercial enterprises, and MIGA which guarantees foreign investment in developing countries.

- United Nations Development Programme for technical assistance and training through the World Tourism Organization as its executing agency.

- European Union for technical assistance and training.

- Regional development banks such as the Inter-American Development Bank, Asian Development Bank and African Development Bank for financing commercial enterprises such as hotels.

- Bilateral aid sources from individual countries. Some countries have a policy for assisting in tourism.

- Non-governmental organisations (NGOs) and volunteer agencies, some of which are involved in small-scale community-oriented tourism development

- Private international capital sources for private capital investment

Financing of particular projects may be from a combination of sources. Each country and area should devise a strategy for financing tourism development and attracting investment in tourism which best suits its circumstances and needs.

HUMAN RESOURCE DEVELOPMENT FOR TOURISM

Having properly qualified persons to work in all aspects of tourism is essential for successful tourism development. Even with the best of tourist facilities, qualified personnel are required to provide the quality level of services that tourists expect and are paying for. Local authorities should assess needs in their areas for the qualified personnel available when and where required as part of the tourism planning and development process. Developing the human resources for tourism requires a systematic approach:

- Surveying and evaluating the present utilisation of personnel in tourism and identifying any existing problems and needs, for example, upgrading the skills of some personnel.

- Projecting the future personnel needed based on the number of personnel required in each category and skill level of employment.

- Evaluating the total human resources that will be available in the future. This involves examination of the number of persons in the area who will be seeking employment in the future, and the educational qualifications of these persons.

- Determining education and training needs of the personnel required and formulating the education and training programmes needed to provide the qualified personnel.

All types of tourism personnel must be considered in manpower development:

- Hotel and catering operations and management personnel including front office and reception, housekeeping, food and beverage service, food production (cookery) and maintenance.

- Tour and travel operations and management personnel including ticketing, tour programming and tour guiding. Vehicle drivers will also be needed.

- Government tourism management officials including planning and development, marketing, application of industry standards, statistical research, information services and other functions.

- Artisans, entertainers, sports directors and other specialist personnel.

Training is needed for basic skills, advanced skills, supervisory and management levels in all categories. Also special tourism sensitivity training is often required of customs and immigration officials, taxi drivers and retail clerks. **Figure 22** shows a model tourism human resource development planning table which can be adapted for use in the local area.

Training approaches include organisation of short courses for existing tourism personnel (these may be in-country or in other countries), regular training programmes in hotel, catering and tourism training institutes or general vocational institutes, university tourism programmes, study tours and on-the-job attachments. Often, large international hotels will provide their own in-house training but this will not be sufficient to provide all the training needs in hotel and catering, especially for the smaller enterprises. Commonly, a hotel, catering and tourism training institute will be established in the tourism area if there is sufficient local need. Such institutes require considerable capital investment and technical resources to be developed properly, and often need outside assistance for initial development and operation. Also, an existing vocational school can develop a tourism department. Determining training needs should always consider upgrading training of existing personnel which is often required.

Each local area will need to assess its tourism education and training needs and determine how to satisfy these. If there are suitable national or regional training institutions, the local authorities may want to encourage some local persons to attend these. If the local area is expected to develop a substantial tourism sector, it may be justified to develop a local tourism training institute or a tourism department in an existing vocational school or polytechnic. The tourism office should co-ordinate closely with the private sector tourism enterprises to develop the most suitable education and training programme. The tourism office will also need to explore opportunities for its own staff to receive the training they need in tourism management, often through regional, national or international programmes. The World Tourism Organization can assist the tourism office in identifying suitable education and training institutions and programmes internationally, including short-term programmes on tourism management.

INVOLVING LOCAL COMMUNITIES IN TOURISM DEVELOPMENT

As has been emphasised throughout this guide, it is essential to involve local communities in the tourism development process. By involving local communities, they will understand tourism, be better able to cope with this new development in their area and participate in its benefits, and therefore more likely support tourism. Also, local communities know their areas and societies best and may have good ideas on tourism development and how they can participate in it. Tourism can bring economic benefits to local communities, both through employment and income generated to local residents and through improvement to community infrastructure, facilities and services. Because tourism is often a new activity in their areas, however, local communities need guidance on their participation in tourism.

Tourism awareness programmes, described in Section 7, should include local community awareness. More specifically, organisation of a steering committee to advise on preparation of the tourism plan, as was indicated previously, should include community spokesmen. If a tourism development project, such as a resort or ecotourism project, is being considered in a particular place, efforts should be made to involve the communities in that place. Meetings should be held with community residents and especially the local traditional and religious leaders to explain the benefits and problems of tourism, discuss tourism development approaches that could be used in the area and review the various ways in which the communities and their residents can participate in and benefit from tourism. A consensus should be reached with the communities on the planning approaches for tourism in their area and a programme formulated for local involvement. When the alternative and final plans and programmes are prepared in co-operation with the communities, they should be carefully reviewed at com-

Figure 22

MODEL TOURISM HUMAN RESOURCE DEVELOPMENT PLANNING TABLE

Job Classification	Existing Employment	Vacant Positions	Projection of New Positions Year 5 Year 10	Attrition Factor	Total Manpower Needs
HOTEL AND CATERING					
Administration					
Manager					
Assistant Manager					
Marketing Manager					
Chief Accountant					
Assistant Accountant					
Secretary					
Reception/Front Office					
Front Office Manager					
Receptionist					
Assistant Receptionist					
Reservation Clerk					
Cashier					
Switchboard Operator					
Head Porter					
Porter					
Housekeeping and Laundry					
Executive Housekeeper					
Assistant Housekeeper					
Room Maid					
Head Linenkeeper					
Head of Laundry Service					
Laundry Worker					
Restaurant and Bar					
Restaurant Manager					
Head Bartender					
Assistant Restaurant Manager					
Head Waiter					
Barman					
Assistant Waiter					
Cashier					
Kitchen					
Executive Chef					
Assistant Chef					
Cook					
Cook Assistant					
Maintenance					
Building Maintenance Engineer					
Gardener					
Cleaner					
Note Specialized Personnel may be required, such as hairdresser, entertainer, recreation leader, etc.					
TOUR AND TRAVEL OPERATIONS					
Agency Manager					
Head of Ticketing					
Head of Tour Programs					
Sales Manager					
Ticketing Clerk					
Tour Leader					
Tour Guide					
Cashier					
Driver					
TOURISM MANAGEMENT					
Director of Tourism					
Chief of Marketing					
Chief of Planning and Development					
Marketing and Promotion Specialist					
Public Relations Officer					
Tourism Planning Specialist					
Tourism Statistician					
Tourist Facility Standard Specialist					
Tourism Training Specialist					
Tourist Information Service Clerk					

munity meetings and agreed to by the communities. In addition to their receiving benefits from tourism, the responsibilities of the communities in developing tourism should be stressed, for example, the need for local conservation measures being applied.

Techniques for bringing benefits of tourism to local communities will need to be determined for each local situation, but general approaches include the following:

- Give priority to employment in the tourism enterprises being developed for local residents. This will usually require special training programmes for local people and, in some backward communities, may even require that remedial basic education in reading, writing, mathematics and hygiene be given in order for the students to be qualified to take the hotel, catering and tourism courses. Foreign language training may also be needed.

- Assist local entrepreneurs to establish small-scale tourism enterprises through technical assistance and small business loans. After the tourism enterprises are started, they will need to be monitored and continued assistance provided if necessary.

- Improve basic infrastructure, such as roads, water supply, electric power and waste management for the communities, as part of the infrastructure development programme for tourism development.

- Apply techniques for some of the revenue from tourism, such as admission fees to parks and archaeological/historic sites, to be used for improving general community facilities and services such as schools and medical clinics.

- If local crafts are produced in the communities, organise the craftsmen to produce and sell items to tourists. This may require special training and development of sales outlets, and guidance on maintaining a good quality level of the crafts.

- If the local communities have traditional dance, music or drama, encourage them to organise performances for tourists, but still maintaining the authenticity of the performances.

- If the local economy is based on agriculture or fishing, develop a programme to use these products in the tourism enterprises without depriving the communities of their own food supply. This may require improving the quality of local products, ensuring a steady and reliable supply and developing marketing and delivery mechanisms.

- Encourage the tourism enterprises to use to the extent possible local products in the construction and furnishings of the tourist facilities, but without creating any environmental problems.

- Organise some community-based tourism projects such as village tourism and ecotourism as were described in Section 4 of this guide.

In some areas, community residents may be dependent on local natural resources, such as wildlife and land for agriculture, that also need to be conserved as both tourist attractions and for ecological reasons. Encroachment into protected areas to clear land for agriculture and poaching of wildlife for meat or sale of animal parts is a common problem in many places. In these situations tourism should be used to provide alternative jobs and income for the residents so that they will not have the need to violate the protected areas, and can be prohibited from doing so. Also some of the admission fees to the parks can be transmitted to the nearby villages so they receive benefits from tourism. Other economic activities can also possibly be developed to provide alternative income for the residents involved. There has been considerable experience accumulated on these community-based conservation initiatives, especially in several countries in Eastern and Southern Africa

There must be continuous monitoring of community involvement in tourism areas and the attitudes of local residents to tourism development. This monitoring will detect which community programmes are successful and should be retained and perhaps expanded, and whether there are problems with other programmes which require remedial action and perhaps re-orientation or discontinuation.

MARKETING AND PROMOTION OF TOURISM

Marketing and promotion of tourism for an area is essential to inform prospective tourists about the area and persuade them to visit it. A comprehensive, integrated tourism plan for an area must include a marketing component. Conducting the market analysis as an essential element of the planning process was described in Section 3 which emphasised the importance of relating the tourist markets and tourism resources of the area. In the sustainable development approach, the targeted markets should be ones which will tend to respect and be sensitive to the local environment and society. Carrying capacity analysis of the area is an important factor in deciding the upper limit of tourists to attract. Based on the market analysis, a marketing plan is prepared.

The first step in preparing the marketing plan is formulation of the marketing objectives and strategy. The marketing objectives will be represented by the market targets of the types and numbers of tourists, and their length of stay, that were established in the market analysis. These targets are set for short, medium and long-term periods. The marketing strategy is then formulated based on the objectives. The strategy sets forth the most effective approach for achieving the marketing objectives, and is concerned with:

- The image of the area to be conveyed.

- Any obstacles to be overcome.

- The relationship of marketing efforts to certain major attractions or facility development such as a resort.

- The types of promotional techniques to be used.

- The scheduling of promotional efforts to the various market sources.

An important element of marketing is providing information services to tourists before and after they arrive in the area. In a newly developing tourism area that is not known to prospective tourists, it is important to develop and convey an appropriate image of the area, usually based on its primary attractions combined with availability of suitable facilities and services. The image conveyed should approximate the reality so that tourists who visit the area are not disappointed and do not take home a poor impression of the area. Even if facilities and services are still limited, an image, for example, of an unspoiled natural environment and adventure of discovery can be conveyed in order to get tourism started. Promotional literature should note deficiencies in the area so that tourists know what to expect. If specialised tourist markets are being sought, such as for special interest, ecotourism and adventure tourism, selective and 'niche' marketing techniques will need to be applied.

If no comprehensive tourism plan that includes a market analysis has been prepared for the area, but the community still wishes to carry out marketing activities for existing tourism development, then a basic marketing approach needs to be applied. **Figure 23** presents an approach that communities can use in marketing their attractions. This approach involves the following steps:

- Conduct an inventory of existing tourist attractions and activities and assess potential attractions that could be marketed. Competition with other similar destinations should be evaluated.

- Clarify community tourism and general development and conservation objectives, including economic, environmental and sociocultural considerations.

- Estimate possible levels of the market demand and carrying capacity of the local area and reconcile these two figures.

- Assess existing and planned tourist facilities and services and related infrastructure including access to the area.

- Determine the potential tourist markets that can be attracted as related to the tourist attractions.

- Determine market segments and market targets.

Identifying potential target markets involves several considerations in addition to the type of local attractions and activities and community development objectives. Knowledge about the geographic locations of the markets is important with respect to transportation access and cost of travel to the destination area. Also, demographic and behavioural characteristics of market segments should be analysed. These include motivation for travel, value systems of the target groups, their specific interests, and their age-sex, marital status, education, income levels and occupation profiles.

Based on the market targets, promotional techniques can be established and a promotion programme prepared. Whether prepared as part of the comprehensive plan or a separate marketing study, the promotion programme is based on the market targets (marketing objectives) and marketing strategy. This requires knowledge of distribution channels and the various promotion techniques available. A promotion programme is usually pre-

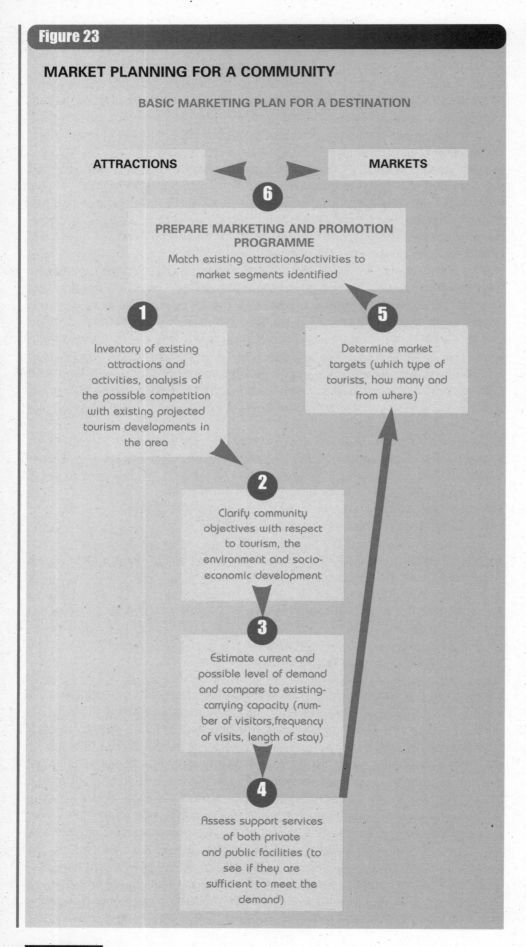

Figure 23

MARKET PLANNING FOR A COMMUNITY

BASIC MARKETING PLAN FOR A DESTINATION

ATTRACTIONS　　　　**MARKETS**

6

PREPARE MARKETING AND PROMOTION PROGRAMME
Match existing attractions/activities to market segments identified

1
Inventory of existing attractions and activities, analysis of the possible competition with existing projected tourism developments in the area

5
Determine market targets (which type of tourists, how many and from where)

2
Clarify community objectives with respect to tourism, the environment and socio-economic development

3
Estimate current and possible level of demand and compare to existing-carrying capacity (number of visitors, frequency of visits, length of stay)

4
Assess support services of both private and public facilities (to see if they are sufficient to meet the demand)

pared for a three to five year period and specifies by year the types of promotion techniques to be undertaken and their estimated costs. Often there is the need to maintain continuity of particular techniques over a period of several years in order for them to have maximum effectiveness. Continuing costs, such as maintenance of local information offices, should be included in the programme.

There are many different types of promotion techniques and they need to be used selectively based on the marketing strategy. The commonly applied techniques include the following:

- Preparing promotional material (called collateral material) of brochures, posters, maps, postcards and travel agency manuals, and distributing these to travel agents, tour operators and the tourist consumers. This is the most widely used technique. Now Internet is being widely used to disseminate information about an area.

- Preparing audio-visual material, such as slide and video shows, for use in travel seminars and other types of presentations. This is also a commonly used technique.

- Advertising in newspapers, magazines, radio and television aimed at the tourist consumers, and in travel trade publications aimed at the travel trade. This can be expensive and should be used carefully.

- Attending tourism trade fairs, many of which are held annually throughout the world, and setting up exhibits and meeting the travel trade. This is usually done at the national or regional level but local areas can send participants and exhibits on these missions.

- Undertaking special promotional trips to the market countries in order to contact travel agents and tour operators, and often arranging travel seminars for the travel trade These seminars usually use audio-visual presentations.

- Inviting and hosting visits by travel agents and tour operators so that they can directly experience the tourist attractions, facilities and services of the area. This is a common practice but can be expensive and usually requires co-operation from hotels and local tour operators in providing accommodation and transportation.

- Inviting and hosting travel writers and photographers, and encouraging travel articles about the area being published in newspapers and magazines in the tourists' home countries or in international media. Authors of commercial tour guide books should also be encouraged to visit the area.

- Preparing and publishing travel guides and general information books about the area, if these are not available commercially. These books can be sold to recover the costs involved.

An important factor in a successful promotion is the message content. It must tell the target markets what they need to know to make a travel decision. If possible, promotional messages should be tested first to determine their effectiveness before making large investments in the production of collateral material. It is important to be careful and accurate about the information conveyed. False, exaggerated or misleading statements can result in dissatisfied tourists and even lead to legal problems. **Figure 24** presents a checklist for evaluating promotional material such as an information brochure.

The results of promotional activities must be measured to determine which ones are effective and which need to be modified or dropped. Some techniques can be directly measured but most general techniques are difficult to assess. Often special surveys must be made of tourists, travel agents and tour operators to determine how they learned about the area.

In preparing marketing strategies and promotion programmes, local authorities should review the marketing plans of their national and regional tourism offices. Local marketing should then be designed to complement the national and regional programmes. Often the local authorities can induce national and regional tourism offices to include their area in the national and regional programmes. Local governments may not have experience in promotion and their budgets are limited for experimentation in promotional techniques. Often the most effective approach that they can use, at least initially, is to contract a public relations or advertising type firm to prepare and implement a promotional programme for the area.

Competent firms can prepare the marketing plan and provide advice on the best promotional approaches to use, and then pursue implementation of the promotion programme or certain aspects of it.

In addition to the promotion carried out by the government tourism office, promotion is undertaken by individual tourism enterprises for their own operations. In order to be effective both in terms of results and cost, there should be close co-ordination between the government tourism office and the private sector so that there is not duplication of efforts and consistent messages are conveyed. Implementing promotion programmes can be expensive and may be beyond the financial resources available to the local government. An approach that is being used in some areas is to organise a joint promotion board that receives funding from both the government tourism office and the private sector and includes representatives of both the government and private sector. This board prepares comprehensive promotion programmes according to common objectives and then carries out the promotion. The private sector can still promote their own enterprises if they wish.

An essential function of the marketing department of a tourism office is to provide information services to tourists. Some tourists will contact the office before their arrival in the area to obtain information and many others will seek information after they arrive. The collateral material referred previously, especially brochures, maps and guide books, can also be used as information material. This material should be written in the languages of the country markets targeted for promotion.

The best approach to providing information services in an area is to establish a tourist information centre, as was described in Section 4, that has a central and accessible location. The information centre contains information material and information officers to answer questions, ideally in various languages, exhibit maps of local attractions and facilities. It is often a hall for audio-visual presentations, guides and other information books for sale, perhaps craft items for sale, a snack bar and toilets. If the tourism area is large, a main centre can be established in the major city or staging area near the tourists' point of arrival and smaller information centres located elsewhere. A tourist information counter should be set up in the airport arrival area if most tourists arrive by air. Information material can also be made available at hotels, restaurants and major attraction features.

Figure 24

CHECKLIST FOR EVALUATING PROMOTIONAL MATERIAL

Printing is cheaper and easier. The result: we are inundated with paper, and in order to survive, we mostly ignore the messages unless something jumps off the page, grabs us and hollers, "This message is what you need!".

The following checklist will help you develop printed material that will grab your readers. But there is no guarantee they will actually read, save and respond to your message.

	Yes	No
Have you clearly identified the audience for this printed piece?	O	O
Have you surveyed materials from your competitors? Will your material compete effectively?	O	O
Have you determined your distribution methods and requirements before creating your design and deciding how many to print?	O	O
Is the size appropriate for the method of distribution ? Will it fit in the display rack (4" by 9" is standard) or mailing envelope?	O	O
Have you designed the material with your target audience in mind? For instance, have you avoided small print if your major audience is seniors?	O	O
Does the cover identify a benefit - visually or through a key word or phrase?	O	O
Do the printed materials reflect your true image? A slick city.style brochure is inappropriate for a remote rustic village. But so is a photocopied version on gaudy yellow paper.	O	O
Is there continuity among all of your printed materials? Do they look as though they are representing the same community? Consider color, design, slogan, logo, typeface, overall impression.	O	O
Have you used less expensive designs for materials with a short shelf life, such as calendars and eating guides?	O	O
Have you a color scheme that appeals to your audience?	O	O
Have you presented facts and eliminated puffery? Cliches, superlatives, and blatant distortion have no place in your materials. Focus on uniqueness.	O	O
Are headlines and picture captions well written?	O	O
Avoid the trendy. Have you come up with something tremendously clever? Check it out with strangers. Learn from their reactions.	O	O

Source: Rural Tourism Marketing, The Rural Tourism Center, State Tourism Office, California, USA, 1957.

Questions for Discussion

IMPLEMENTING TOURISM IN YOUR AREA

1. Identify the respective roles of the public and private sectors, NGOs and any other organisations in your area to develop tourism?

2. Does your area or community have a legal procedure for adopting tourism plans?

3. Does your community have zoning regulations to guide and control land uses and development standards? If so, are these suitable for tourism or should they be modified to guide the physical development of tourism?

4. Does your area have engineering standards for infrastructure and a building code and are these adequate for tourism development?

5. Does your community have a development or action programme into which tourism projects and actions can be integrated, or is a separate programme for tourism necessary?

6. What types of projects and actions do you consider need to be included in a tourism development action programme?

7. What are the sources of public funding likely to be available for tourism development in your area? Will these be adequate for developing tourism? If they are not adequate, where can additional sources of funding be sought?

8 Are private sector sources of funding likely to be available and adequate for developing tourism enterprises? If not, how can additional private sector funding be found? Are there investment incentives offered in your area to attract private investment in tourism development?

9. Would it be appropriate to establish a public corporation for developing certain tourism projects in your area?

10. What techniques can be applied in your area to encourage community involvement in tourism development, and especially for local communities to receive benefits from tourism?

11. If there is existing tourism development in your area, are the tourism personnel properly qualified? If not, what additional types of qualifications do they need?

12. Are there any training institutions for tourism in your area? If so, what types of training programmes are offered? How could these be improved?

13. Based on the present and future training needs, what type of overall tourism education and training approach and programme would you propose for your area?

Questions for Discussion

14. Does your area currently have a tourism marketing programme? If so, do you consider this effective or are improvements needed?

15. What do you propose as being suitable marketing objectives and strategy for your area? How do these relate to national and regional tourism marketing objectives and strategies that affect your area?

16. What types of promotional techniques do you recommend for your area based on the types of tourism and tourist markets you wish to develop? How are these co-ordinated with national and regional promotional techniques that affect your area?

17. Are any tourist information services provided in your area and, if so, how could these be improved? What is the best approach to providing information services in the future?

18. What are the most appropriate respective roles of the government tourism department and the private tourism enterprises in marketing of tourism in your area?

19. How can co-operation be achieved between government and the private sector in marketing tourism in your area?

20. If any tours are organised in your area, are these logically routed and interesting to tourists and, if not, what would be the logical organisation of new tours?

AN OVERVIEW

Maintaining the sustainability of tourism requires managing environmental and socio-economic impacts, establishing environmental indicators and maintaining the quality of the tourism product and tourist markets. With good planning, development and management of tourism, negative impacts of tourism can be minimised, but tourism development must be continuously monitored, and actions taken if problems arise in order to ensure that tourism remains sustainable.

maintaining the sustainability of tourism

SECTION 6

There is a close relationship between tourism and the environment. Tourism can generate both positive and negative impacts depending on how well it is planned, developed and managed. Various environmental protection measures must be employed including developing adequate transportation and utility systems, applying environmentally suitable land use and site planning principles and development /design standards, carefully managing visitor flows and controlling visitor use at attractions.

There can also be positive and negative socio-economic impacts resulting from tourism. However, socio-economic impacts are generated by all types of development and especially exposure of traditional societies to modern media. Tourism is only one of several types of outside influences on an area. Various policies can be exercised to minimise negative and reinforce positive impacts. A basic approach that has already been emphasised is encouraging community participation in tourism. Important approaches to enhance economic benefits are to establish strong linkages between tourism and other economic sectors and to encourage local employment in, and ownership and management of tourism enterprises, as well as to increase tourist expenditures especially on locally produced items.

Important techniques to mitigate negative sociocultural impacts are to: maintain the authenticity of local arts and crafts; ensure that residents have affordable access to tourist attractions and facilities; prevent overcrowding of attractions; educate residents about tourism; inform tourists about local customs and dress codes; and apply strict controls on trafficking and use of drugs, crime and prostitution if these are problems in the area. It may be necessary to organise a structured sociocultural programme.

Even though tourism projects have been planned environmentally and the environmental impact assessment procedure is applied to specific projects, tourism development must still be monitored to ensure that no serious negative impacts are taking place. The technique now used to monitor impacts is that of establishing environmental indicators for each tourism area or development site. These indicators are periodically measured and if problems are emerging, corrective action can be taken. The quality of the tourism product must be maintained and the product periodically revitalised so that tourist satisfaction levels remain at a high level and the tourist markets are retained. It may be desirable in some areas to eventually modify the tourism product and re-orient the tourist markets.

MANAGING ENVIRONMENTAL IMPACTS

There is a close relationship between tourism and the environment in several respects. Many features of the natural and built environment are attractions for tourists and tourism can help achieve protection of the environment. Tourist facilities and infrastructure constitute one element of the built environment, and tourism development and tourist use of an area can generate both positive and negative environmental impacts. Finally, the overall level of environmental quality of the tourism area is important for both residents and tourists.

Many types of environmental impacts can be generated by tourism development and tourist use of the environment. If tourism is well planned, developed and managed, the impacts can be positive. Appropriate tourism development:

- Helps justify and pay for conservation of important natural areas and wildlife including marine environments because these are attractions for tourists.

- Helps justify and pay for the conservation of archaeological and historic sites because these are attractions for tourists.

- Helps improve the overall environmental quality of areas because tourists like to visit places that are attractive, clean and not polluted. Improvement of infrastructure for tourism also contributes to better environmental quality.

- Increases local environmental awareness when residents observe tourists' interest in conservation and realise that protecting the environment is important.

If tourism is not well planned, developed and managed, it can generate several types of negative environmental impacts including:

- Water pollution resulting from improper waste management of sewage and solid waste systems of hotels and other tourist facilities. Water pollution includes pollution of river, lake and coastal waters from sewage outfall lines and of ground water by seepage of waste materials.

- Air pollution resulting from excessive use of internal combustion vehicles in tourism areas and inadequate exhaust systems on these vehicles. Aircraft generate some air pollution.

- Noise pollution resulting from tourist activities and tourist vehicles including aircraft movements.

- Vehicular and pedestrian traffic congestion generated by tourists at popular attraction and facility sites.

- Unattractive landscapes (visual pollution) resulting from several factors: poor design of hotels and other tourist facilities; badly planned layout of facilities (poor land use and site planning); inadequate landscaping of tourist facilities; use of large and ugly advertising signs; and obstruction of scenic views by tourism development.

- Littering of the landscape by tourists and defacing of features by graffiti and vandalism.

- Ecological disruption of natural areas and disturbance of wildlife by overuse and misuse by tourists and inappropriate tourism development. Coastal, marine, mountain and desert environments, all important types of tourism areas, are particularly vulnerable to ecological damage. In coastal areas, for example, onshore development may increase erosion and runoff with sedimentation into the coastal waters which smother and kill coral reefs.

- Damage to archaeological and historic sites by overuse and misuse by tourists and inappropriate tourism development.

- Environmental hazards such as erosion, land slippage, damage from high waves, flooding, earthquakes etc. and land use problems resulting from poor planning, siting and engineering of tourist facilities, as explained in Section 3.

Specific types of environmental problems take place in different environments. **Figure 25** lists the types of negative impacts that can occur in coastal tourism areas.

This guide has stressed that protection of the environment and minimising environmental impacts must be considered throughout the sustainable tourism planning process. **Figure 26** lists some basic guidelines for improving the tourism-environment relationship. As has been referred to, an especially important basic principle is not exceeding the carrying capacity levels of sites. Other environmental protection measures that were referred to and should be integrated into tourism planning, development and management process include the following:

- Develop properly designed utility (infrastructure) systems of water supply, electric power, waste management and drainage for tourist facilities. Energy saving techniques such as use of solar energy and conservation of water use should be incorporated into tourist facility development.

Figure 25

POTENTIAL IMPACTS OF TOURISM IN COASTAL ENVIRONMENTS

POTENTIAL IMPACTS	TOURISM DEVELOPMENT CAUSES
Coral Reefs and Seagrass	
• Physical damage to coral reefs and collection of organisms	Reefwalking, collection of shells & coral, boat anchoring, diving
• Increase in freshwater runoff & sediments	Land clearing for construction
• Introduction of waterborne pollutants (nutrients & pesticides)	Waste water outfalls of poorly treated sewage in coastal waters
Estuaries/lagoons	
• Encroachment	Land filling for siting of structures
• Changes in sedimentation patterns	Placement of structures on beaches and over water
• Changes to the salinity regime	Fresh water runoff
• Introduction of waterborne pollutants	(see coral reefs)
• Destruction of submerged and fringing vegetation	Runoff, sedimentation, recreational use
• Inlet modifications	Harbour maintenance, siting of buildings and structures
• Loss of fishery habitat increased	Land use modifications, runoff, sedimentation, pollution
Mangroves	
• Changes in freshwater runoff, salinity regime and tidal flow patterns	(see coral reefs)
• Excessive siltation	Construction, sewage discharge
• Introduction of pollutants	(see coral reefs)
• Conversion of mangrove habitat & overharvesting of resources	Used as a tourism development site
Salt Marshes (tidal flats)	
• Degradation of bird habitat & seed collection sites	Discharging wastes, fish alternation of site for tourism
• Obstruction of storm-water runoff	Alteration of tidal flats for tourism development
Barrier Beaches, Sand Dunes & Spits	
• Sand mining	For construction purposes
• Erosion	Improper siting of structures
• Dune migration	Removal of natural vegetation

Source: Adapted from Environmental Guidelines for Coastal Tourism Development in Sri Lanka. Kate Sullivan et al, ed. Coastal Conservation Department, Sri Lanka.

Figure 26

GUIDELINES FOR IMPROVING THE TOURISM-ENVIRONMENT RELATIONSHIP

1. Environmental considerations should be fully incorporated in tourism development plans, especially with respect to air and water (potable and recreational) quality, soil conservation, the protection of natural and cultural heritage and the quality of human settlements.

2. Tourism goals should be based on the carrying capacity of sites and environmental sustainability and compatible with regional development, social concerns, and land use planning.

3. Decisions should be based on the fullest available information with respect to their environmental implications. Environmental impact assessment (EIA) should be applied to proposed major developments, to evaluate the potential damage to the environment in light of forecasted tourism growth and peak demand. Alternative sites for development should be considered, taking into account local constraints and carrying capacity. This capacity includes physical, ecological, social, cultural, and psychological factors.

4. Adequate environmental measures at all levels of planning should be defined and implemented. Particular attention should be paid to peak demand, sewerage, solid waste disposal, noise pollution, and traffic density control. In the most endangered zones, comprehensive improvement programmes should be formulated and implemented.

5. Incentive schemes should be applied in both the public and private sectors to spread tourism demand over time and space in order to make optimal use of accommodation.

6. Regulatory power should be used to limit developments in sensitive areas, and legislation should be drawn up to protect rare, endangered, and sensitive environments.

7. As part of general efforts to prevent environmental degradation, but also in its own interests, the travel and tourism industry should oppose (by refusing to take part in unsustainable developments, withdrawing investment, lobbying governments and industry bodies, working together with NGOs);

- dumping of untreated sewage into the sea
- unsustainable fishing, including blasting, long lining and whaling
- coral mining and collecting
- unsustainable forestry, tropical forest clearance for ranching and clear-cutting
- unsustainable framing methods
- siting of nuclear power plants near tourism areas
- siting of tanker shipping lanes near bathing beaches
- continued use of CFCs

and support with finance, complementary investments, lobbying for:

- efforts by governments and NGOs to protect the environment
- measures to reduce power station and factory emissions
- installation of oil containment and clean-up equipment at strategic locations to fight oil spills
- direct negotiations with representatives of indigenous peoples before undertaking any developments which would affect their land or way of life.

Source: Tourism, Ecotourism, and Protected Areas. Héctor Ceballos-Lascurain. International Union for Conservation of Nature and Natural Resources (IUCN): Cambridge, UK. 1996.

- Develop adequate road and other transportation systems, with emphasis on use of non-polluting public transport systems. Electric shuttle buses, for example, can be used in resorts and parks. Proper maintenance of tourist vehicles is important to prevent air pollution as well as promote safety.

- Apply environmentally suitable land use and site planning principles, zoning regulations, development standards and architectural design in tourism areas. Control of advertising signs and undergrounding of utility lines are important in maintaining an attractive environment.

- Provide open space, parks and environmentally suitable landscaping in tourism areas and resorts.

- Carefully manage visitor flows at tourist attraction features. At fragile sites, the number of visitors may need to be limited or completely prohibited at certain times, or even year-round. For some important sites, the techniques of modelling can be used, that is to build a replica of the feature for tourists to visit with prohibition of tourists at the original site.

- In natural areas, prohibit tourists from cutting flowers or trees in camping and trekking areas or from collecting rare plant and animal species, and control disturbance of wildlife. Hunting and fishing should be allowed only under carefully controlled conditions so that the animal populations are maintained at sustainable levels appropriate to their habitats. In deserts, off-road recreational vehicle use should be limited to a few specified areas or completely prohibited.

- In marine environments, several types of controls are important: places where ship bilge cleaning operations are allowed; use of motorised boats in environmentally sensitive areas; collection of live sea shells; collection or damage of coral; disturbance of nesting turtles; use of boat anchors in coral-bottom bays; mining of beach sand and coral for construction purposes; excessive fishing and removal of decorative fish for sale. Boat piers should be properly designed so that they do not lead to erosion or other problems.

There are other types of control measures which should be applied in particular tourism areas depending on their characteristics. **Figure 27** indicates an example of some environmental impact factors and mitigating actions for East Africa.

With respect to visitor use controls, it is important to inform tourists about the controls and why they must be applied. If tourists understand why the controls are necessary, they will more likely abide by them. However, it is also necessary to patrol the tourism area to monitor visitor use, warn tourists if they are violating the regulations, and establish penalties for those who commit serious violations. The importance of applying community-based conservation programmes to encourage protection of natural areas by local residents was emphasised in Section 5. If local residents receive some benefits from tourism based on the protected areas, they will more likely respect them and not engage in practices such as poaching animals or encroaching into the areas with agricultural activities.

Tour operators have an important role in managing environmental impacts and maintaining the sustainability of tourism through promoting appropriate types of tourism products and tourist activities and other actions. Annex 6 sets forth environmental guidelines for European tour operators which can also be a guide for operators elsewhere. These guidelines are also useful for local authorities when setting standards for tourism development in their areas.

MANAGING SOCIO-ECONOMIC IMPACTS

Social, cultural and economic impacts, both positive and negative, are all closely related. As is the case with environmental impacts, tourism planning should consider socio-economic impacts throughout the planning process so that the benefits are maximised and problems are minimised. However, continuous monitoring and management of these impacts are still necessary as is emphasised in Section 7 of this guide.

Tourism is sometimes criticised for its negative sociocultural impacts, especially in small and more traditional communities. Although tourism can bring some negative impacts, it should be recognised that all types of new development bring impacts, including exposure to outside influences such as modern media of newspapers, magazines, radio and television. Residents who have travelled outside their home areas also bring back new ideas and behavioural patterns. Tourism is usually only one of the various types of development and outside influences in an area that generate impacts.

It is important to understand the types of socio-economic impacts and how to reinforce the positive impacts and prevent or mitigate the negative ones. Positive socio-economic impacts include the following:

- Economic benefits and improvement of living standards in an area. Economic benefits are measured in terms of:

- Employment and income from working in the tourism sector, both directly in hotels, restaurants, tour and travel operations and retail shops and indirectly in the supplying sectors such as agriculture, fisheries, craft production, manufacturing and construction. There is also induced employment generated by expenditures made by the direct and indirect employees, for example, in retail shops.

- Stimulation of local entrepreneurship through establishment of local tourism enterprises, and development of skills to work in tourism that can be transferred to other activities.

- Foreign exchange earnings at the national level. At the regional and local levels, tourism generates income from outside the area.

- Contribution to government revenues at all levels including the local level if there are local types of taxes related to tourism. These revenues can be used to improve community facilities and services and local infrastructure.

Figure 27

MANAGING NEGATIVE IMPACTS IN PROTECTED AREAS

The guiding principle for sustainable tourism development is to manage the natural and human resources so as to maximize visitor enjoyment and local benefit while minimizing negative impacts upon the destination site community and local population. This requires an objective assessment of potential negative impacts and a thoughtful analysis of how this potential can be controlled. The following chart identifies many tourism development factors and their negative impacts and suggests mitigating or corrective action. Corrective action is based upon the assumption that the negative impact has already occurred. Better planning earlier in the process obviously would be even more desirable.

FACTOR INVOLVED	NEGATIVE IMPACT ON ENVIRONMENTAL QUALITY	POSSIBLE MITIGATION OR CORRECTIVE ACTION
Overcrowding	• environmental stress on humans • changes in animal behaviour in wildlife areas	• Limit visitor access • expand carrying capacity
Overdevelopment	• creation of rural slums • habitat loss • destruction of vegetation • land scars and watershed interference • aesthetic impact of power lines	• disperse visitors to other areas and attractions • upgrade and rehabilitate • apply land use planning zoning regulations
Noise pollution	• irritation to wildlife local residents and visitors • Limit visitor access	• conduct awareness campaign • establish regulations
Litter	• wildlife depends upon garbage • aesthetic clutter • health hazards	• conduct awareness campaign • establish regulations • provide litter containers at appropriate places
Vandalism	• Mutilation and destruction of facilities • loss of irreplaceable historic and cultural treasures	• conduct awareness campaigns • establish regulations • increase surveillance
Airport noise	• environmental stress to humans and animals	• consider altering take-off and landing patterns • establish land use controls near airports
Overcrowded roads	• environmental stress to humans and animals	• increase availability of public transportation
Off-road driving	• soil vegetation and wildlife damage	• Limit access • establish or improve enforcement regulations
Powerboats	• disturbance of wildlife especially during nesting season • noise pollution	• restrict access and use • implement environmental education programme
Fishing and hunting	• competition with natural	• restrict access

	predators	• implement environmental
	• resource depletion	education programme
Foot safaris	• disturbance of wildlife	• install or modify trails
	• trail erosion	• restrict access and use
		• implement environmental
		education program
Souvenir collection	• removal of endangered natural items such as coral, shells, horns, rare plants	• environmental education and awareness campaign
	• disruption of natural processes	• legal restrictions
Firewood collection	• habitat destruction	• environmental education and awareness campaign
	• mortality of small wildlife	• use alternative fuels
Unauthorized feeding of wildlife	• behavioural changes and dependency	• environmental education and awareness campaign
Construction of billboards	• spoils the view	• establish regulations

Source: Protected Areas in East Africa & Training Manual, James Thorsell. Gland, Switzerland: IUCN.

- The multiplier effect of tourism serving as a catalyst for the expansion of other local economic activities such as agriculture, fisheries, crafts, etc. as indicated above on employment generation. **Figure 28** illustrates how the multiplier effect works.

- Improvement of infrastructure financed in part by tourism, which also serves local communities.

- Conservation of the cultural heritage of an area. The cultural heritage of an area including dance, music, drama, crafts, fine arts, dress, customs, traditions, ceremonies and other cultural patterns might be in danger of becoming lost in the face of modern development. Because these cultural patterns are often important attractions for tourists, tourism provides the justification and helps pay for their conservation. Also, tourism helps support museums, theatres and other cultural facilities and activities which are used by residents as well as tourists.

- Renewal of pride by residents in their culture when they observe tourists taking an interest in and wanting to learn about their culture.

- Cross-cultural exchange of tourists and residents learning about one another's culture. This can lead to mutual understanding and acceptance and peaceful relationships among people of different cultural backgrounds.

Tourism's role in the conservation of archaeological and historic sites and other cultural monuments was emphasised in the previous section on environmental impacts.

Figure 28

THE MULTIPLIER EFFECT

The following chart demonstrates how tourism spending flows through the economy.

Tourists spend for:	Second round of expenditures:	Ultimate beneficiaries (a partial
Lodging	Wages and salaries	Accountants
		Appliance repairpersons
Food	Tips and gratuities	Architects
		Artisans and craftspeople
Beverages	Payroll taxes	Arts and crafts suppliers
		Athletes
Entertainment	Commissions	Attorneys
Clothing		Auto servicepersons
	Music and entertainment	Bakers
Gifts and		Bank workers
souvenirs	Administrative and general	Butchers
	expenses	Carpenters
Personal care,		Cashiers
medicines,	Professional services	Charities
cosmetics		Cinema and video makers/distributors
	Purchase of food and beverage	Clerks
Photography	supplies	Clothing manufacturers
		Cooks
Recreation	Purchase of goods for resale	Cultural Organizations
		Dairies
Tours,	Purchase of material.s and	Dentists
sightseeing,	supplies	Department store owners/workers
guides and local		Doctors
transportation	Repairs and maintenance	Education providers
		Electricians
Miscellaneous	Advertising promotion and	Engineers
	publicity	Farmers
		Fisherpersons
	Utilities	Freight forwarders
		Furniture makers
	Transportation	Gardeners
		Gift shop operators
	Licenses	Government workers
		Grocers
	Insurance premiums	Health care providers
		Housekeeping staff
	Rental of facilities and	Insurance workers
	equipment	Laundry service providers
		Manufacturing workers
	Interest and principal payments	Office equipment suppliers
	of borrowed funds	Painters
		Petrol stations
	Income and other taxes	Plumbers
		Porters
	Replacement of capital assets	Printers and publishers
		Recreation equipment, sales/rental
	Return to government	Resort owners, operators and workers
		Restaurant owners, operators
		Road maintenance workers
		Sign makers
		Transport workers
		Utilities, providers of and repairpersons
		Waters and waitresses
		Wholesale suppliers

Leakage: When the private or public sector purchases goods or services from outside the community, that money is no longer subject to the multiplier effect and the economic benefits leak out of the community.

Source: World Tourism Organization

Possible negative socio-economic impacts can include loss of potential economic benefits if tourism is not closely linked with other local economic activities and there is much importation of goods and services used in tourism. If tourist facilities and services are owned and managed by people outside the area or if local persons are not employed in tourism, there can be both loss of local benefits and resentment of tourism by residents. If not developed in a planned and gradual manner, tourism development may lead to local increases in the price of land and goods. Also there can be economic and employment distortions generated by tourism if tourism is concentrated in only a few places without corresponding development (of any type) in other places of the area, or if tourism attracts persons from other activities such as agriculture. Overdependence on tourism in an area may result in decline of other economic activities and create an unbalanced economy.

Uncontrolled development of tourism may result in negative sociocultural impacts. Overcrowding of local attractions and amenity features by tourists may be resented by residents who cannot enjoy these features. Over-commercialisation of the arts and crafts may lead to loss of authenticity of dance, music, drama and crafts. The 'demonstration effect', especially on young people, of imitating the dress and behavioural patterns of tourists may generate social problems and loss of cultural identity. Misunderstandings and conflicts can arise between residents and tourists because of differences in languages, customs, religious values and behavioural patterns. Tourists may be irritated and have a bad impression of the local area if they are hassled by vendors and touts persistently selling goods and services. Local social problems of drugs, alcoholism and prostitution may be exacerbated by tourism, although tourism is seldom the basic cause of these problems.

An important general planning policy to reinforce positive impacts and mitigate negative ones is to encourage community involvement in tourism, as has already been emphasised in this guide. Residents should understand tourism, participate in the decision-making on tourism planning, development and management, and have the opportunity to receive benefits from tourism. It is also important that a form and scale of tourism that is appropriate for the local environment and society (social carrying capacity) be developed. Medium and large resorts may be appropriate and acceptable in some places, small-scale development will be more suitable in other places while urban areas can typically accept more intensive development of tourism. An important policy is to develop tourism on a gradual basis which allows residents time to adapt to it, as well as time to monitor the social (and environmental) impacts and take any remedial measures if problems arise.

A basic policy to enhance the local economic benefits of tourism is to establish strong cross-sectoral linkages to other economic activities. Tourism should make maximum use of locally produced products and services such as food items, building materials, décor and furnishing, arts and crafts and local tour and travel services. In fact, use of local goods and services can make tourism in an area a more interesting and educational experience for tourists, giving them a sense of being in a unique place. Programmes may be required, however, to encourage stronger cross-sectoral linkages. There may be the need, for example, to improve the quality of agricultural products for tourism use, provide a steady and reliable sources of supply of the products and establish efficient marketing and transportation mechanisms. Some importation of goods, at least from other parts of the country or region is, however, often necessary and inevitable to provide a good quality tourism product. Tourism can still bring benefits to the area even though some goods and services are imported.

Also important is to seek ways to encourage local ownership and management of tourist facilities and services, such as offering low-interest loans and other incentives to local investors and to advise potential local entrepreneurs in establishing tourism enterprises. However, for larger-scale tourist facilities, it may be necessary to rely on some outside capital and management when these factors are limited locally. Priority should be given to employment of local persons in tourism and it may be necessary to organise special programmes to train local people to work effectively in tourism. If the attractions and access are available, tourism should be encouraged in economically depressed areas where employment and income are particularly needed.

Tourist expenditures can be increased by various techniques. The area can provide more local shopping opportunities by producing a greater variety of crafts and speciality items such as fashion clothing. The number and variety of local tourist attractions and activities can be expanded and local tour routes extended, which will lead to an increase in the length of stay of tourists and their expenditures. Sometimes this can be achieved by simply improving the information to tourists on the variety of tours and activities available.

Some other approaches to reinforce positive socio-economic impacts and mitigate negative ones include:

- Maintain the authenticity of local dance, music, drama, arts and handicrafts in traditional areas through training programmes and quality controls.

- Ensure that residents have affordable access to tourist attractions through such techniques as providing lower admission fees to residents, free access to residents on certain days and free access to student, youth and elderly groups. Public access should be provided to beaches as was described in Section 3.

- Apply visitor use organisation and control measures to prevent overcrowding of tourist attractions, as was described in Section 4.

- If local incomes are low, provide special inexpensive or subsidised accommodation and recreation facilities for residents of the area.

- Educate residents about tourism (public awareness programmes) and tourists about local customs (tourist behaviour code) as is described in Section 7.

- Design hotels and other tourist facilities that reflect local architectural styles to integrate them into the local cultural environment, as was explained in Section 3.

- Through techniques of selective marketing, attract the types of tourists who will respect the local environment and cultural traditions and want to learn about them.

- Apply strict controls on trafficking and use of drugs, crime and prostitution and especially child prostitution, if these are existing or potential problems are in the area. Warn tourists not to visit areas where there are high crime rates.

- Control hassling of tourists by local vendors and persons selling goods and services. Craft markets can be developed in tourism areas where vendors can rent stalls at low rates and mobile selling discouraged.

In newly developing tourism areas, it may be useful to establish a sociocultural programme that will provide a structured approach for using tourism to help achieve cultural conservation. At the same time, these cultural expressions can serve as significant tourist attractions. **Figure 29** presents a model organisational structure for a sociocultural programme that can be adapted for use in local areas.

USE OF ENVIRONMENTAL INDICATORS

Even though environmentally planned and developed, an environmental impact assessment prepared and visitor use controls have been applied, unanticipated environmental problems may arise in the future. For tourism areas which have not had the benefit of good planning and development, there may be existing environmental problems that need to be analysed and resolved. For managing environmental impacts, a technique now being used is that of establishing and applying environmental indicators. These indicators relate to both the natural and built environment as well as sociocultural considerations and economic costs and benefits..

The World Tourism Organization has produced a first set of environmental indicators of sustainable tourism for tourism managers' use (see Bibliography). These indicators measure information on the impacts of tourism in an area to show whether positive impacts are taking place as expected and negative impacts are being prevented. If positive impacts are not reaching expectations, the indicators will show this. If negative impacts are arising, the indicators will identify them before they become serious. Environmental indicators can be used by decision-makers in taking action where necessary to reinforce positive impacts and prevent or mitigate negative ones. Each local authority should establish a list of environmental indicators that measure the most important types of impact for the particular area involved based on the objectives of tourism development in the area.

Which indicators will be relevant to tourism manager's decision-making depends on the destination's characteristics and the development objectives. For example, if the main objective at a destination is to preserve specific attributes of the natural environment so that it can continue to be enjoyed, key indicators may be:

- Those which measure the size of protected areas.

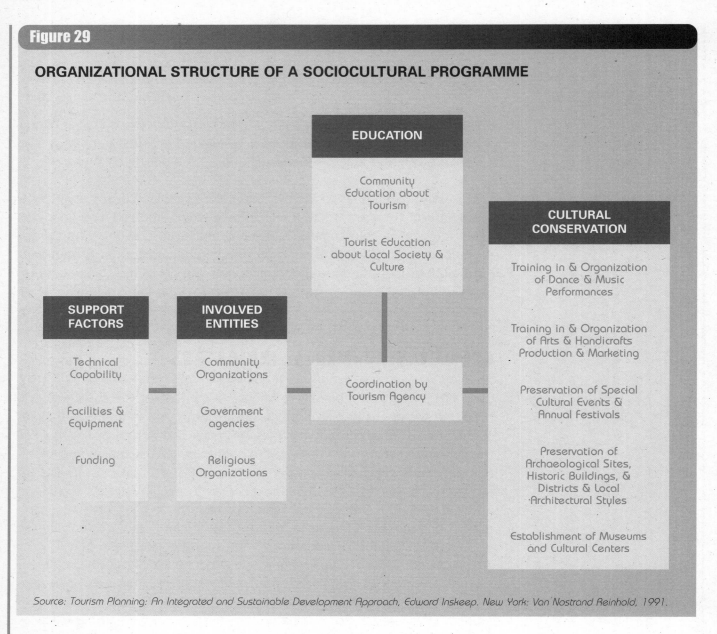

Figure 29

ORGANIZATIONAL STRUCTURE OF A SOCIOCULTURAL PROGRAMME

EDUCATION

Community Education about Tourism

Tourist Education about Local Society & Culture

CULTURAL CONSERVATION

Training in & Organization of Dance & Music Performances

Training in & Organization of Arts & Handicrafts Production & Marketing

Preservation of Special Cultural Events & Annual Festivals

Preservation of Archaeological Sites, Historic Buildings, & Districts & Local Architectural Styles

Establishment of Museums and Cultural Centers

SUPPORT FACTORS

Technical Capability

Facilities & Equipment

Funding

INVOLVED ENTITIES

Community Organizations

Government agencies

Religious Organizations

Coordination by Tourism Agency

Source: Tourism Planning: An Integrated and Sustainable Development Approach, Edward Inskeep. New York: Van Nostrand Reinhold, 1991.

- Those which measure the loss in biodiversity (flora and fauna) and the degradation of ecosystems

If the objective is to maintain the quality of an historic site and its popularity as an attraction, key indicators may be:

- Those which measure preservation of the integrity of the site.

- Those which measure the satisfaction levels of visitors and the trend in number of visitors.

If the objective is to bring the benefits of tourism to particular communities based on local tourist attraction features, key indicators may be:

- Those which measure local economic benefits of tourism such as employment, income and locally owned tourism enterprises.

- Those which measure maintenance of the quality of attractions and visitor satisfaction levels.

Figure 30 sets forth Core Indicators of Sustainable Tourism that are generally applicable to most tourism areas. Annex 7 lists supplementary specific indicators that can be used for different tourism environments. However, it is important that each area develop a set of indicators that it considers most relevant to its own situation. Indicators may vary for different tourism sites within local areas.

MAINTAINING THE TOURISM PRODUCT AND TOURIST MARKETS

Maintaining the sustainability of tourism also requires maintaining the quality and sometimes enhancing the tourism product of tourist attractions, facilities, services and related infrastructure. Physical maintenance of attractions, facilities and infrastructure is essential to ensure that these remain in good condition. Effective management ensures that service quality is maintained. The importance of applying tourist facility quality standards was reviewed in Section 3 while management of quality and maintaining the vitality of the tourism sector are examined in Section 7. By maintaining quality standards of the tourism product, tourist satisfaction levels are kept at high level and the tourist markets sustained.

Figure 30

CORE INDICATORS OF SUSTAINABLE TOURISM

INDICATOR	SPECIFIC MEASURES
1. Site Protection	Category of site protection according to IUCN* index
2. Stress	Tourist numbers visiting site (annum/peak month)
3. Use Intensity	Intensity of use - peak period (persons/hectare)
4. Social Impact	Ratio of tourists to locals (peak period and over time)
5. Developing Control	Existence of environmental review procedure or formal controls over development of site and use densities
6. Waste Management	Percentage of sewage from site receiving treatment (additional indicators may include structural limits of other infrastructural capacity on site such as water supply)
7. Planning Process	Existence of organised regional plan for tourist destination region (including tourism component)
8. Critical Ecosystems	Number of rare/endangered species
9. Consumer Satisfaction	Level of satisfaction by visitors (questionnaire based)
10. Local Satisfaction	Level of satisfaction by locals (questionnaire based)
11. Tourism Contribution to Local Economy	Proportion of total economic activity generated by tourism only

COMPOSITE INDICES

A. Carrying Capacity	Composite early warning measures of key factors affecting the ability of the site to support different levels of tourism
B. Site Stress	Composite measure of levels of impact on the site (its natural and cultural attributes due to tourism and other sector cumulative stresses)
C. Attractiveness	Qualitative measure of those site attributes that make it attractive to tourism and can change over time

* International Union for Conservation of Nature and Natural Resources

Source: *What Tourism Managers Need to Know: A Practical Guide to the Development and Use of Indicators of Sustainable Tourism.* World Tourism Organization. 1996.

MAINTAINING SUSTAINABLE TOURISM IN YOUR AREA

1. Are there any significant positive or negative environmental impacts of tourism or general development in your area? If so, what are these?

2. How could present negative impacts be mitigated? How could they have been prevented?

3. Is the infrastructure in your area sufficiently well developed in order to prevent environmental problems if tourism is developed? What new or improved infrastructure needs to be developed for tourism in order to prevent environmental problems in the future?

4. If there are any protected natural areas such as nature or marine parks and reserves in your area, how should visitor facilities be developed and visitor use managed to prevent negative environmental impacts?

5. If there are any archaeological or historic sites in your area, how should visitor facilities be developed and visitor use managed to prevent negative environmental impacts?

6. Are there adequate regulations adopted to protect natural and archaeological/historic sites in your area? If such regulations have been adopted, are they being applied and is there adequate staff assigned to enforce the regulations?

7. Are there any community-based conservation approaches being applied in your area to encourage protection of natural areas?

8. What do you consider are the important socio-economic benefits of tourism in your area at present if there is some tourism development? And in the future, based on proposed tourism development?

9. Are there any socio-economic problems resulting from tourism or other types of development in your area? If so, what are these and how could they be mitigated? How could they have been prevented?

10. Are there any problems in your area resulting from the behavioural patterns of tourists at present if there is some tourism development? Are they likely to occur in the future based on proposed tourism development?

11. Do residents have access to tourist attraction features in your area? Are there affordable tourist facilities available to residents?

12. Are existing tourist facilities and services in your area owned by residents or outsiders? Would it be possible for more facilities and services to be owned by residents?

13. Are there any problems of congestion at tourist attractions in your area at the present time, or likely to be in the future?

14. Are most of the existing employees in tourism in your area from the local communities?

Questions for Discussion

15. If there is some tourism developed in your area, what is your estimate of the percentage of local goods and services used in tourism, and what percentage is from outside the community? What types of tourism goods and services are imported into your area?

16. In what ways could the economic benefits of tourism be enhanced in your area, for both present and future development?

17. Is the authenticity of local crafts and performing arts being maintained in your area? If authenticity is being lost, what techniques could be used to revitalise these arts and crafts?

18. Do you believe that a structured programme to encourage cultural conservation would be appropriate in your area? If so, what should this programme emphasise?

19. List the most important types of environmental indicators that should be applied in your area generally and for specific tourism sites?

20. If there is some existing tourism development in your area, are the tourist markets being sustained or are there market problems and what are the reasons for these problems?

AN OVERVIEW

Effective management of the tourism sector by local authorities, in co-operation with the private sector and NGOs, is essential. Tourism management has several functions including policy and planning, co-ordination with other government agencies, establishing and administering standards for tourist facilities and services, marketing, education and training, maintaining the vitality of the tourism sector, monitoring and responding to crisis situations when they arise.

managing the
tourism sector

SECTION

7

Government tourism departments are typically organised into planning and development, marketing services, statistics and research and education and training. Often a semi-autonomous body is established to handle promotion and other functions. It is important for the private tourism sector to be organised into associations. These can serve several purposes including representing industry's interests to the government, maintaining quality control of their own tourism enterprises and sponsoring training and special events.

A basic tool for effective management is establishing a computerised tourism management information system (TMIS). The TMIS provides a data base for marketing research, development activities and monitoring the progress of tourism. The TMIS should contain all types of information on tourism in the area including tourist arrivals and their characteristics, tourist attractions, facilities and services, economic data and environmental and sociocultural impacts. Monitoring of tourism is an essential management function. Monitoring should be applied to plan implementation, tourist markets, development projects, the environmental and socio-economic impacts of tourism, tourist satisfaction levels and other factors. The vitality of the tourism sector must be maintained through quality controls and adjustments made to the tourism product and tourist markets based on changing circumstances.

Public education on tourism must be carried out, especially in newly developing tourism areas. This takes the form of tourism awareness programmes which utilise various techniques and media. Especially important is to institutionalise tourism awareness by incorporating it in the school curriculum. Tourists should be informed about local customs. An effective approach is to prepare a tourist behaviour code which is given to all tourists as a brochure and included in tour guide presentations.

Maintaining the safety and security of tourists is vital in managing tourism. There are various types of safety and security problems. The local area should have a safety and security plan and programme and the tourists themselves must assume some responsibility for their own safety and security. As a tourism area matures, coping with saturation of tourist attractions and facilities often becomes a major concern. There are various techniques to increase the tourist capacities of sites: the dispersal of tourists throughout the tourism area and reducing seasonality are important approaches. However, maximum capacities can be reached and the number of tourists must then be limited. Responding to crises situations such as natural disasters is an important management function. Achieving sustainable tourism requires the co-ordinated support and management of all parties involved—government, private sector, NGOs and the tourists.

FUNCTIONS AND ORGANISATION OF TOURISM MANAGEMENT

Continuous and effective management of the tourism sector by local authorities in an area is essential for the sustainable success of tourism. Tourism management has several functions:

- Establish tourism development policy and prepare tourism plans, and co-ordinate all aspects of implementation of the plans' recommendations. Tourism management is responsible for revising the plans as needed and for improvement and expansion of the tourism product in order to maintain the vitality of the tourism sector.

- Co-ordinate with the physical planning (sometimes called the town and country planning department) and the environmental protection agencies on review and taking action on tourism-related development proposals, to ensure that these reflect the plan's recommendations on type and location of development and meet suitable development and design standards. If no planning or environmental protection agencies exist, then the tourism office has this sole responsibility for review and action.

- Co-ordinate with the transportation and other infrastructure agencies to ensure that infrastructure is available for tourism when and where needed and, that the infrastructure meets acceptable standards as much as possible.

- Co-ordinate with other government agencies in tourism-related development, including those agencies responsible for protected areas (nature parks and reserves) and conservation of archaeological and historic sites. Co-ordination with the public health and safety agencies is important. Close co-operation must be maintained between the public and private sectors to achieve co-ordinated tourism development. If local NGOs are involved in developing tourism, such as community-based and eco-tourism projects, tourism management must co-ordinate with them.

- Establish and administer standards for tourist facilities and services including licensing and inspection requirements and a hotel classification system if one exists, and ensure that appropriate standards are adopted and applied by other involved agencies such as tourist vehicle safety standards.

- Carry out tourism marketing activities, including research when necessary and provision of information services. At the local level, this will require co-ordination in marketing with the regional and national tourism offices.

- Establish standards and programmes for education and training of local persons to work in tourism, to supplement education and training programmes that may be available at the regional and national levels. There may be a need to establish either a public or private local hotel, catering and tourism training institute. Formulating and carrying out tourism awareness programmes and informing tourists about local customs is an important aspect of the education and training function.

- Monitor tourism development and ensure that tourism stays on track in terms of development and marketing including meeting the market targets. Monitoring and other research activities requires maintaining a tourism data base in the form of a tourism management information system.

- Respond to crisis situations when they arise. Many types of unexpected crises affecting tourism can happen such as a local natural disaster, disease epidemic that affects tourists, serious accident or crime problem affecting tourists, sudden decline in an important tourist market or temporary political instability.

Depending on the local situation there may be other functions that must be assumed in integrated tourism management.

Both the government and private sector tourism enterprises should be organised for tourism management. As was emphasised in Section 5, in newly developing tourism areas, the government must usually adopt a strong role in tourism management even though the private sector is expected to develop the commercial facilities and services of tourism. Government tourism offices, whether at the national, regional and local levels, typically are organised according to functional activities, as follows:

Planning and Development:

development policy and planning, co-ordination of plan implementation and development, establishment and administration of facility and service standards.

Marketing Services:

market planning and promotion, co-ordination of marketing with national and regional tourism departments, operation of local tourist information offices.

Statistics and Research:

statistical collection, compilation and reporting, operation of the tourism management information system, conducting of special surveys and research studies.

Education and Training:

manpower planning and programming, establishment and administration of training standards, operation of training programmes and institutions if needed in the local area, and carrying out a public tourism awareness programme.

If plan implementation is an important function, sometimes a separate plan implementation unit is established. This can be either under the planning and development section or by reporting directly to the Director of Tourism. Many places have organised a separate semi-autonomous entity for marketing services and sometimes other management functions related to implementing tourism development. Assigning marketing to a separate body, such as a promotion board, offers the advantage of its being more responsive to market trends. Also, it allows for the possibility of co-ordinating with the private sector on joint promotion activities. Although somewhat autonomous, the board must be held accountable for effective use of its funds, usually through an annual review of its programme and expenditures by the tourism department.

Because tourism is a multi-sectoral activity, it is essential that maximum co-ordination be maintained between the tourism department and other government agencies and between the public and private sectors. This can usually best be achieved by establishing a tourism advisory committee with representation from government agencies, the private sector and other relevant organisations.

Effective tourism management by the government requires a technically qualified and motivated staff with effective leadership, adequate office facilities and equipment, logistical support of vehicles and resources for special activities such as conducting tourist surveys. Promotional activities in particular, need sufficient financing. Thus, the tourism department must be properly funded by the government or by other sources to carry out its functions.

If the government needs to become involved in the development of resorts or other types of tourist attractions or facilities, a commonly used approach is to organise a public development corporation. This entity is funded by the government, but functions as an independent company subject to government review. When the private sector becomes more mature in the area, the public corporation may sell its assets to private investors.

Private sector tourism enterprises commonly organise themselves into associations and should be encouraged to do so. These can be separate associations for each type of enterprise such as hotels, restaurants, tour and travel agents and transportation services such as rental cars. In a small area, the enterprises may combine groups such as hotels and restaurants or combine into one association for all tourism-related enterprises. If the local tourism enterprises in a newly developing tourism area have not taken the initiative to organise themselves, then the government tourism department may need to encourage and assist them in their organisation.

Private sector tourism associations serve several important functions:

- Providing a forum for discussing and resolving common problems of the tourism enterprises.

- Making co-ordinated recommendations to the government tourism department for improvements in the tourism sector.

- Providing representation on tourism-related boards and committees.

- Conducting research and training for their member enterprises.

- Establishing and maintaining adequate facility and service standards of their members, and taking action on members who do not meet standards or violate codes of conduct.

- Sponsoring special events, either by themselves or in co-operation with the tourism department.

The private sector has an essential role in promoting sustainable tourism being practised by tourism enterprises. As an example of private sector initiative, **Figure 31** sets forth guidelines for operators of nature safaris that were established by the industry. **Figure 32** presents the Ten Commandments on Ecotourism that have been adopted by the American Society of Travel Agents and are distributed to tourists. This statement recognises that tourists also have a responsibility in maintaining sustainable tourism and tourists' responsibility should be encouraged by the private sector.

As referred to in Section 5, NGOs can often perform an important role in developing community-based tourism projects such as eco- and village tourism. They are also often involved in conservation projects which relate to tourism. Tourism management should encourage NGO involvement if their projects are compatible with tourism policy and planning, and co-ordinate with these NGO activities.

TOURISM INFORMATION SYSTEM AND MONITORING

An essential tool for effective tourism management is a tourism management information system (TMIS). The TMIS provides a data base for conducting marketing research, decision-making on development activities and monitoring the progress of tourism. The data will provide the basis for making improvements needed to the tourism product. The information system should be computerised to establish the data base according to statistical standards recommended by the World Tourism Organization. It should be compatible with any TMIS that has been established by the regional or national tourism departments so that information can be easily exchanged. If feasible, the local TMIS should be networked with the national and regional systems.

The types of information to be placed in the TMIS at the local level include:

Figure 31

GUIDELINES FOR OPERATORS OF ENVIRONMENTALLY RESPONSIBLE SAFARIS

- State your commitment to conservation in brochures and other pre-departure information.

- Conduct orientations on conservation and cultural sensitivity before and during the trip. Arrange to meet with wildlife rangers for all safari tours, not only for special-interest tours.

- Provide guidance about endangered species products sold in souvenir shops and why to avoid them in pre-trip printed materials. During the trip patronize only appropriate craft concessions that sell locally-produced goods that benefit the local economy. Explain when it is or isn't appropriate to bargain or barter for goods.

- Build in a contribution to a conservation, cultural, or archaeological project. Or encourage donations by clients directly to the reserve, wildlife service or non-profit projects. Or adopt a specific project. Or hold a fund-raising drive to donate specific equipment or meet other needs. Or give a membership to a wildlife organization as a tour benefit. Provide an opportunity for clients to see what project they are helping to support.

- Equip clients with information to help minimize any negative impact (e.g., don't wear bright colors, distracting patterns, or perfume, don't smoke, talk loud or crowd the animals with more than five vans at one time, stay on the roads). This encourages clients not to pressure drivers to break the rules of the reserve. Stop at the visitors center. Provide copies of park rules for clients and explain why they are important.

- Discourage negative social ramification.s that result by giving candy and inappropriate gifts to children along the route. If there is something to donate, have the tour guides give it to a village elder or school teacher to distribute.

- Ensure that ground operators train drivers/guides. Give recognition or monetary awards for safety excellence and sensitivity to the rules of the reserve. Ask drivers to turn off the engine to alleviate noise and reduce diesel fuel exhaust when viewing wildlife or scenery.

- Follow up the safari with newsletters and information on wildlife appeals. Give a progress report on any adopted project the client helped support. Ask clients for feedback after the safari .

- Explain your commitment to the environment to tour operator colleagues, travel agents during office visits and at trade shows, and in-bound ground operators. Share ideas on materials, driver training, and ethical standards for the industry. By presenting the company's commitment as a competitive selling point, it can serve to heighten awareness and others may be persuaded to evaluate their practices, too.

Source: Wildlife Tourism Impact Project materials, Lauric Lubeck, California, USA, 1991.

- Tourist arrivals in the area and their characteristics such as nationality and for domestic tourists, which region of the country they live, purpose of visit, age-sex groups, general type of occupation, general income levels, whether travelling in groups and individually, and any other characteristics relevant to tourism research in the local area. Length of stay and seasonal patterns of tourist arrivals should be recorded.

- Satisfaction levels of tourists in the area and their attitudes toward the type and quality level of attractions, facilities, services and infrastructure.

- Tourist attractions by type and location, number and types of visitors at specific attractions in the area, and the seasonality of visitor arrivals to the various attractions.

- Accommodation by type, number of rooms, location, room rates and quality level. As accommodation units are expanded or upgraded, that information is recorded.

- Other tourist facilities and services, such as restaurants, tour and travel services and rental car agencies, by type, size, location and quality level (if that is relevant).

Figure 32

ASTA'S TEN COMMANDMENTS ON ECOTOURISM

Whether on business or leisure travel:

1. **Respect the frailty of the earth.** Realize that unless all are willing to help in its preservation, unique and beautiful destinations may not be here for future generations to enjoy.

2. **Leave only footprints. Take only photographs.** No graffiti! No litter! Do not take away "souvenirs" from historical sites and natural areas.

3. To make your travels more meaningful, **educate yourself about the geography, customs, manners, and cultures of the region you visit.** Take time to listen to the people. Encourage local conservation efforts .

4. **Respect the privacy and dignity of others.** Inquire before photographing people.

5. **Do not buy products made from endangered plants or animals,** such as ivory, tortoise shell, animal skins and feathers. Read "Know Before You Go," the U.S. Customs list of products which cannot be imported.

6. **Always follow designated trails.** Do not disturb animals, plants or their natural habitats.

7. Learn about and **support conservation-oriented programs and organizations** working to preserve the environment.

8. Whenever possible, **walk or utilize environmentally-sound methods of transportation.** Encourage drivers of public vehicles to stop engines when parked.

9. **Patronize those** (hotels, airlines, resorts, cruise lines, tour operators and suppliers) who advance energy and environmental conservation; water and air quality; recycling; safe management of waste and toxic materials; noise abatement; community involvement; and which provide experienced, well-trained staff **dedicated to strong principles of conservation.**

10. Ask your ASTA travel agent to **identify those organizations which subscribe to ASTA Environmental Guidelines for air, land and sea travel.** ASTA has recommended that these organizations adopt their own environmental codes to cover special sites and ecosystems.

An example of how a professional travel association can promote environmentally sustainable tourism.

Source: American Society of Travel Agents

- Tourism economic data such as expenditures of tourists, employment generated by type, contribution of tourism to the local economy and government revenues and other relevant economic measures.

- All types of environmental and sociocultural impact information.

- Other data such as the results of monitoring development and development proposals can be recorded on the TMIS.

To obtain the data and keep it current, procedures need to be established for receiving regular reports from accommodation facilities on the number and types of guests they have, from tourist attractions on their visitor admissions, licensing agencies and other sources. Conducting special surveys of tourists will be essential to obtain their characteristics, travel patterns in th area and satisfaction levels. Tourist surveys can either be continuous or periodic and carried out on a sampling basis. Periodic surveys should be made of tourism enterprises to obtain employment figures and other information.

Local tourism data should be published on a periodic basis and distributed to other government agencies, tourism enterprises, investors and other interested parties. Especially important as the data base is maintained, is to determine trends that are taking place in the area.

An essential management function is monitoring all aspects of tourism including several factors:

- The progress being made on implementing the tourism development plan and programme.

- The tourist markets including tourist arrivals and their characteristics, their length of stay and seasonal distribution, number of visitors at tourist attractions and to what extent the market targets are being met.

- The progress of specific development projects.

- Economic, environmental and sociocultural impacts of tourism and overall environmental quality of the tourism areas.

- Tourist satisfaction levels.

- Education and training of persons to work in tourism.

- Any other relevant factors of tourism in the area.

Monitoring will determine whether tourism is on track and will detect any problems before they become serious, so that remedial action can be taken. More generally, monitoring provides the basis for evaluating whether the overall tourism development policy, plan and programme are effective for achieving the development objectives, or whether adjustments need to be made. Effective tourism planning and development require some experimentation with different approaches to determine which are the most appropriate for the area.

Monitoring should be undertaken on a formal, structured basis according to scheduled programme. The tourism management information system will be an important tool to use in the monitoring process. Special surveys and field visits need to be conducted to obtain all the information needed for monitoring. Surveys should include interviews and meetings with residents of the tourism areas to ascertain their attitude towards and participation in tourism development. Surveys of tourists and tourism enterprises are necessary. The results of the monitoring process should be published for use by government agencies and the private sector.

MAINTAINING THE VITALITY OF THE TOURISM SECTOR

Another important function of tourism management is maintaining the vitality of the tourism sector, as was referred to in Section 6. Basic to the vitality of an area is maintaining and, where necessary, improving quality stan-

dards. The government must establish minimum standards of health, safety and comfort and, in a newly developing tourism area, must offer guidance to tourism enterprises on quality standards. However, quality control is the basic responsibility of the tourism enterprises for their own benefit and productivity through maintaining a satisfied tourist clientele.

A report on quality control of tourism products and services by the WTO (Quality Control of Tourism Products and Services, 1988) concluded that:

The tourism enterprise or organisation must move from simply monitoring to managing quality on the basis of a quality policy. This process must be developed within the staff. Quality control must serve first to correct problems identified as such and systematically to seek improvements for reasons of competitiveness or good economic health. Quality policy is therefore everyone's business and must be oriented toward at least four objectives:

- Improving the quality of products and services.

- Improving productivity.

- Improving the quality of life in the workplace.

- Improving the organisation and methods of work.

Figure 33 sets forth a checklist that tourism managers can use in assessing the quality of service being offered by local tour operators and how effectively they interact with local communities.

Even after the tourism development plan, or its first stage, is implemented, tourism management should not become complacent that the tourism product is the most suitable one for the future. Changing tourism trends may render some products obsolete and the expectations of tourist markets may change. Also some areas may wish to upgrade their tourism product and re-orient their tourist markets over time to achieve a higher quality level of tourism. Also, some attractions may be reaching their saturation (carrying capacity) levels and action will need to be taken to avoid stagnation. **Figure 34** shows, in simple graphic format, what can happen to a tourism area as it matures and the importance of rejuvenation of the area if it is to retain its vitality and sustainability. The most successful tourist destinations over the long-term period are those that are constantly rejuvenating themselves with new and improved attractions and facilities that meet tourists' expectations and compete effectively with other destinations.

The monitoring process provides a basis for determining whether and what type of adjustments need to be made in the tourism product and tourist marketing. Tourist satisfaction levels will need to be monitored and their attitudes toward the tourism product surveyed to determine what improvements are needed. Policy discussions will indicate whether the area wishes to re-orient its product and markets, typically to a higher quality (and higher spending) level than that of the original development patterns which helped get tourism started in the area. Selective visits to other tourism areas will give tourism managers ideas on what is being developed elsewhere including competing destinations. Interviews of tour operators will reveal their perceptions of suitability of the tourism product in the area and how it can be improved. Especially important is for tourism management to keep abreast of new approaches in interpretation of natural and historic/cultural tourist attrac-

Figure 33

CHECKLIST FOR ASSESSING TOUR OPERATORS

	Yes	No
Does the tour operator demonstrate an understanding of heritage and culture of the area visited?	○	○
Does the tour operator assist and encourage clients to respect and appreciate that heritage and culture?	○	○
Does the tour operator respect the natural environment including plants and animals and assist and encourage clients to respect and protect the natural environment?	○	○
Does the tour operator demonstrate sensitivity by portraying local residents honestly in advertising brochures? by respecting religious ceremonies? by encouraging the tour participants to ask permission before photographing local residents?	○	○
Are locally owned and operated lodging facilities used when available?	○	○
Are locally owned and operated food services used when available?	○	○
Are local guides used and trained?	○	○
Is there adequate opportunity for interaction between tour participants and local residents when they may meet as equals to share professional, religious, or cultural interests?	○	○
Are tour arrangements made far enough in advance?	○	○
Are advance arrangements reliable and honored?	○	○
Are local services for tour groups adequately compensated?	○	○

Source: North America Coordinating Center for Responsible Tourism, California, USA.

tions to keep them interesting to tourists and new types of tourist activities such as new forms of special interest, recreation and adventure tourism.

There are constantly changing trends in tourist markets. As these become increasingly fragmented, new specialised markets are emerging. Also, as more countries and regions within countries make economic progress, new geographic markets are emerging, often with their own particular characteristics. Depending on the tourism product in the area, some of these new markets can possibly be tapped by tourism management. Also as saturation levels are reached in the area, re-orientation to a higher quality product and markets will produce the desired economic benefits from a fewer number of tourists. Resorts are also changing, and it is now common practice to 'remodel' and revitalise resorts, often at considerable cost, but necessary to keep them as viable enterprises.

Figure 34

A TOURISM CYCLE OF EVOLUTION

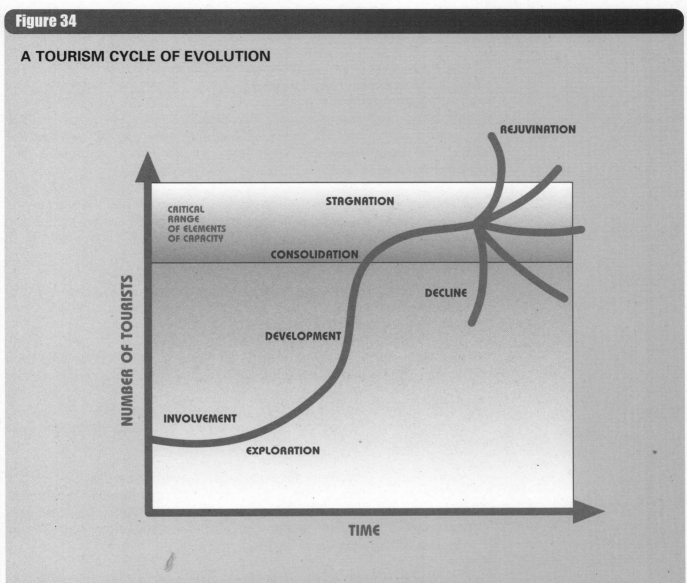

Source: R.W. Butler "The concept f a Tourist Area Cycle of Evolution: Implications for Management of Resources", Canadian Geographer, vol. 24, no. 1, 1980, p.7

EDUCATING THE PUBLIC AND INFORMING TOURISTS

The general public in the local area and especially communities near tourism development sites, must be educated about tourism—its benefits, problems (and how to overcome problems) development plans and programmes, current tourism events, and how to cope with tourists with different cultural and language backgrounds. Particularly important is to expose local residents to ways in which they can benefit from tourism, either directly or indirectly. Raising community awareness about environmental protection of nature areas, conservation of archaeological and historic sites, maintaining traditional arts and crafts, and improving environmental quality is usually an important aspect of public awareness because of the importance of conservation to tourism development.

Public education on tourism takes the form of tourism awareness programmes. These programmes should be prepared initially, often as part of the tourism development plan and programme, when tourism commences in an area and then are pursued on a continuous basis. However, they can be prepared and applied after tourism development has commenced in the area. Public awareness programmes should be systematically prepared based on establishing the objectives of the programme, determining the target groups such as the general public, school students, traditional groups and leaders, government officials, journalists, religious groups and leaders, diplomatic personnel, etc., and specifying the awareness techniques to be used. The basic techniques commonly used in public awareness programmes are as follows:

- Regular radio broadcasts which explain current events and activities in tourism as well as basic concepts. Radio is often the best way to reach a large number of people in traditional and widely dispersed tourism areas.

- Regular or occasional local television programmes on tourism. The programmes often include interviews of persons involved in tourism to make them more interesting.

- Newspaper articles about tourism concepts, events and development projects. There can be a regular weekly or monthly column on tourism.

- Posters, brochures and booklets, designed for wide distribution, which explain tourism. Posters can be graphically designed to be understood even by illiterate persons.

- Instruction in tourism in the local school system, perhaps as part of social science classes. This is the best way to institutionalise exposure to tourism for young people and can include guidance on how students can make a career in tourism. Special presentations can be made by tourism officials to school classes.

- Community and village meetings on tourism with tourism officials invited to make presentations. This is an important approach to use where tourism development is proposed near to the communities, and should include ways in which residents can benefit from tourism. Often a series of meetings is needed, as well as a specific programme on community involvement in the tourism development.

- Publication of a periodic magazine on tourism events, designed for both the general community and organisations and persons directly involved in the tourism sector.

- Public seminars or conferences on specific aspects of tourism. These may be held regularly such as an annual tourism conference in the area.

In newly developing tourism areas, often the awareness and understanding of tourism by public officials including political, religious and traditional leaders is limited. If local authorities do not understand tourism and how it is developed and managed, they may not give full support to developing this sector. Organising seminars and conferences on tourism is often an effective approach to raise awareness of public officials and community leaders. When the area tourism plan has been prepared, this provides a good opportunity to organise a high-level seminar to review the plan and at the same time raise awareness of public officials and leaders about tourism.

In tourism areas where the local cultural traditions and customs are different from those of the tourist markets, misunderstandings often arise as a result of tourists, usually inadvertently, violating some customs which leads to resentment of tourism by residents. It is important that tourists be informed about local customs, dress codes, acceptable social behaviour, how to conduct themselves in religious and sacred places, the local tipping policy, whether bargaining is expected in local markets and shops, courtesies to observe in taking photographs and any other matters relevant to showing respect for local social values and customs. Environmental conservation policies and rules may be included with this information. It may also be necessary in some places to warn tourists about specific local problems such as crime and precautions that should be taken, touting by persons selling goods and services and overcharging tourists in shops.

This information often takes the form of a tourist behaviour code or "do's and dont's for tourists" that can be produced as a simple brochure often with humorous graphic illustrations, and can be included in tourist guide literature. It can also be explained by tour guides.

TOURIST SAFETY AND SECURITY

Safety and security are vital in successfully developing tourism and tourism development and management approaches should incorporate principles of safety and security. Annex 8 reproduces the WTO Resolution from the Experts Meeting on Tourist Safety and Security held in 1994. The WTO publication, Tourist Safety and Security, examines this subject in detail. It identifies risks originating in four source areas:

Human and institutional environment

The risks originating in the human and institutional environment appear when tourists fall victim to common delinquency (theft, pickpocketing, etc.), targeted violence such as rape, organised crime, terrorism, wars and political or religious unrest, and lack of public and institutional protection services.

Tourism and related sectors

Deficient functioning of tourism and related sectors may be responsible for damage to the tourists' personal security, physical integrity and economic interests as a consequence of defects in safety standards in tourism establishments, defects in sanitation and respect for sustainability of the environment, and absence of protection against unlawful interference, crime and delinquency in tourist facilities, fraud in commercial treatment, non-compliance with contracts and personnel strikes.

Individual travellers

Travellers themselves may create problems for their own safety and security, and their hosts as well. These causes include dangerous practices by tourists in sport and leisure activities, driving, food and drink, tourists' previous health condition that may deteriorate while travelling, tourists' behaviour with respect to resident populations or local laws, specific illicit or criminal activity, visits to dangerous areas, and loss of personal effects through carelessness.

Physical and environmental risks

These risks result if travellers are: a) unaware of the natural characteristics of the destination and their effects; b) not prepared from the medical standpoint (vaccinations, prophylaxis); c) not taking the necessary precautions in their eating and hygienic habits; and d) exposed to emergency situations such as natural disasters and epidemics.

Tourism areas at all levels from national to the local level should have a tourism safety and security plan and programme. This plan would include the following elements:

- Identification of potential tourist risks according to type of travel, affected tourism sectors and locations.

- Detection and prevention of criminal offences against tourists.

- Protection of tourists and residents from illicit drug trafficking.

- Protection of tourist sites and facilities against unlawful interference.

- Establishment of guidelines for operators of tourist facilities in the event of such interference.

- Information to be provided to the international travel trade on safety and security issues.

- Organisation of crises management in the event of a natural disaster or other emergency.

- Responsibilities for dealing with the press and other media, at home and abroad.

- Adoption of safety standards and practices in tourist facilities and sites with reference to fire protection, theft, sanitary and health requirements.

- Development of liability rules in tourist establishments.

- Safety and security aspects of licensing for accommodation establishments, restaurants, tour buses, rental cars and taxis.

- Provision of appropriate documentation and information on tourist safety to the public, for both outgoing and incoming travellers.

- Development of policies with regard to tourist health, including reporting systems on health problems of tourists.

- Development of tourist insurance and travel assistance insurance.

- Promotion, collection and dissemination of reliable research statistics on crimes against travellers.

Local authorities should survey the risks to safety and security in their areas and take remedial action where necessary. Especially important is properly applying health and safety standards in accommodation, restaurants and other tourists facilities. No risks can be completely eliminated, and tourists should be informed to take reasonable precautions where some risk is involved. However, every attempt should be made to control crime and harassment against tourists in the tourism areas. A common approach is to organise 'tourist police' in tourism areas. These are specially trained persons who patrol tourism areas, stopping any criminal acts in progress, discouraging harassment of tourists by vendors and touts, answering questions that tourists may have and informing tourists when they are doing something inappropriate. Their presence in the tourism area is in itself a deterrent to crime and harassment.

COPING WITH SATURATION

When tourism has not been carefully planned, or sometimes even with planning according to sustainable development principles, there is the danger that at some point the carrying capacity of either the natural or social environment or infrastructure of a tourism site will be reached. Saturation will occur, and the quality of the tourism product and tourist experience will be depreciated, with consequent environmental and social problems. As quality drops there will be a decrease in tourist satisfaction levels and a decline in tourist markets or shift of markets to less desirable ones. The various types of negative impacts of tourism were described in Section 6.

Saturation levels of tourism sites need to be anticipated and appropriate management strategies applied. If saturation has already been reached, these strategies can also be used to help rejuvenate the area. The three basic strategies to cope with saturation are increasing the site capacity, limiting the number of tourists visiting the site and dispersing the pressure of tourists. These can be applied separately or more commonly, they are applied in combination.

Increasing the capacity of a site can be accomplished through various techniques:

- Expand capacities of utility services such as water supply, electric power, waste management and telecommunications. Conservation measures can be applied to reduce use of water supply and electric power. Recycling techniques can be used to conserve water use.

- Expand capacities of the transportation facilities and services such as roads and parking areas or preferably limit access to the site by private vehicles and provide pollution-free shuttle bus service from peripheral parking lots to the attraction features of the site. It is usually desirable to locate accommodation facilities outside the attraction site.

- If possible, provide high-use attraction features close to the access points of the site to reduce traffic demand to other parts of the site.

- In a large site, such as a nature park, develop more attraction points throughout the site so that no one place becomes too congested. New trails can be established to disperse hikers more throughout the park.

- Provide more group facilities and reduce the number of individual facilities.

- Provide for more efficient flow of tourists through the site without depreciating the tourist experience.

- Educate tourists to make more careful use of the site so that it experiences less deterioration even though the number of visitors increases.

- If there is local resentment of the increasing number of tourists, educate residents about the importance of tourism, ensure that some benefits of tourism accrue to local communities and ensure that attractions and amenity features are available to residents at affordable costs.

- Improve existing facilities, where relevant, to be more appropriately designed and environmentally suitable.

- If the site is small or vulnerable to damage from excessive use, develop a model or replica of the feature nearby which tourists can visit and prohibit tourist access to the original site.

Expansion of capacity normally has a maximum limit beyond which it cannot be increased. If the demand continues growing, then techniques may need to be applied to limit the number of tourists visiting the site, especially at peak periods when capacities are most likely to be exceeded. Several approaches can be used to limit the number of tourists:

- Impose self-limiting measures such as pricing mechanisms of higher room rates and admission fees during the peak period and lower rates and fees during the low season.

- Close certain vulnerable areas, such as environmentally fragile nature areas at certain times to allow for rejuvenation of the ecology or during crucial periods such as animal breeding seasons.

- Limit access to the site such as parking or availability of passenger seating capacity on public transportation.

- Require a reservation system for use of facilities such as camping areas or for admission to the site.

- Establish a maximum number of persons who are allowed on the site at any particular time or a maximum number per day.

- Establish a maximum number of accommodation units such as hotel rooms and camping sites allowed to be developed to serve the site, and control or prohibit construction of new facilities through zoning permit procedures.

Often access to the site is automatically controlled when all accommodation is reserved or transportation passenger seats, such as on airlines or trains, are reserved during the peak periods. Because saturation often occurs only during peak periods, techniques can be used to reduce seasonality of tourist arrivals as is examined below.

Dispersing the pressure of tourists arrivals to particular sites within the tourism area is a common approach. This can be done by developing new attraction features and tourist facility areas if several potential attractions and facility sites are available in the area. For example, as one beach or nature park becomes crowded, other parks can be developed and opened to visitors. Additional historic places can be restored and developed with visitor facilities as the first historic attractions become saturated. Dispersing tourists is also desirable because it distributes the benefits of tourism more in the area. Sometimes, 'man-made' attractions such as theme parks can be developed to distribute tourist use. However, this approach requires substantial public and private investment in infrastructure and development of attractions, facilities and services.

The pressure of tourist arrivals can be dispersed more throughout the year to reduce seasonal peaks of tourist use. This approach also distributes the benefits of tourism more throughout the year. Fortunately, a trend in tourism is for tourists to take more frequent and shorter vacations, often during different seasons of the year, so more tourist markets are available for low-season travel. Several techniques can be used to reduce seasonality:

- Develop tourist attractions and activities that will attract tourists at different times of the year, and especially during the low season. For example, mountain ski resorts can develop summer-time activities such as trekking and horse-riding and hosting conferences and seminars. Beach resorts can host conferences during the low season. Special events such as cultural festivals and sports competitions can be organised during the low season.

- Apply marketing techniques of special promotional programmes during the low season and target certain market groups, such as older and retired people, who can travel at any time of the year.

- Apply pricing mechanisms, as mentioned previously, of higher accommodation rates and admission fees during the peak season and lower prices during the low season.

- Encourage domestic tourism and residents' use of the attractions and facilities during the low season including visits of school and youth groups during this season. Incentives can be provided through offering free or low admission fees to residents during the low season.

CRISIS MANAGEMENT

An important management function is to respond rapidly and effectively to crisis situations. Crises in tourism in an area can result from many sudden problems: natural disasters such as high winds and flooding associated with major storms and earthquakes and seismic waves (tsunamis) that strike tourism areas, epidemics of diseases such as cholera and hepatitis, political unrest and protests, ethnic conflicts and civil wars, violent acts of terrorism that affect tourists, and serious criminal acts against tourists such as murder and rape. Typically the pattern of a tourism disaster is as follows:

• An incident occurs and the media describe the incident in starkest terms, often but not always exaggerating the extent of the crisis.

• Tourists leave the area, tour operators cancel bookings and travel agents stop making sales.

• The destination suffers economically with reduced tourist arrivals and may continue experiencing poor press coverage that magnifies the effects of the incident.

• The destination commences its own media coverage, disseminating an accurate account of the situation.

• Vigorous and often expensive promotion is carried out over time and eventually tourists again visit the destination and tourism resumes its normal pattern.

Local authorities should have a disaster plan for general application in the area. The local tourism office should also have plans for action in the event of a major crisis affecting tourism. These plans should be co-ordinated with national and regional tourism disaster plans. In addition to responding to the crises with respect to the health and safety of tourists, the media must be dealt with in an honest and accurate manner. **Figure 35** lists the basic principles for dealing with the media in a crisis situation. These principals can be applied at both the national and local levels of tourism management. After the disaster is over, the initial information on the disaster has been conveyed to the media and remedial action taken to mitigate the results of the disaster and reduce the possibilities of future similar crises, a promotional campaign can be organised to renew the positive image of the area and eventually attract back the normal flow of tourists.

ROLES IN SUPPORTING AND MANAGING SUSTAINABLE TOURISM

Achieving sustainable tourism requires the co-ordinated support and management by all parties involved. As has been emphasised in this guide, local authorities as well as regional and national government tourism departments, the private sector tourism enterprises, non-governmental organisations (NGOs) and the tourists themselves all have responsibilities in achieving sustainable tourism. **Figure 36** graphically illustrates how ecological and economic sustainability can both be achieved through the co-ordinated efforts of the government, the tourism industry, NGOs and the tourist clients on managing the tourism environment, through regulation where necessary and selective marketing of tourism. **Figure 37** lists the responsibilities of these four groups.

It is important that local authorities establish a strong tourism department under effective leadership, adequately funded and with a competent motivated staff to carry out its tourism management functions. NGOs are becoming increasingly active especially in community-based conservation and development and can give strong support to sustainable tourism. The tourism industry, especially through tourism enterprise associations, must perform an essential role in maintaining good quality standards of facilities, observing environmental protection measures, respecting local cultural traditions and bringing some benefits of tourism to local communities. Tourists, who are becoming more environmentally and socially sensitive, have an important role in selecting environmentally appropriate facilities and services and showing respect for the local environment and society when they travel.

All these parties must closely co-ordinate their efforts and programmes toward reaching common goals in the sustainable tourism development process. With these parties assuming their responsibilities and working together, much progress can be made in achieving sustainable tourism.

Figure 35

PRINCIPLES FOR DEALING WITH THE MEDIA DURING A CRISIS SITUATION

1. Be quick. Information speeds around the globe in a matter of minutes. If you do not provide the information quickly, the media will still report the news, but without the benefit of your input. Your objective must be to have your information figure as part of the first story when an incident occurs at your destination. The objective should be to translate vague and hence harmful impressions of the nature and locations of incidents into a more detailed assessment of risk probabilities at the given destinations.

2. Be honest and factual. National tourism administrations need to have credibility with the media. By their very nature, safety and security events are exceptional. Natural disasters, crime, and health problems do not know international boundaries. If an event occurs at your destination, provide full information—who, what, when, where, how—and add as much background information as possible. Background information will tend to put such events into perspective.

3. Be responsive. Your first press release may generate additional requests for information, background, or interviews. Cooperation with the press can pay long term dividends.

4. Be prepared. The national tourism administration should have a designated person for dealing with the media. That person should be familiar with all information relating to safety and security and should have a data base of all press representatives in the country and principal ones abroad. Overseas tourism offices of the country should replicate this organization. The media will be more understanding if they know the tourism press person and are used to dealing with him or her. If the media are receiving a steady stream of information from the press person, that information will usually be good news, which tends from the start to put emergencies into the context of an exceptional event.

Such policy may help build alliances on information contents based on principles of ethics and openness, by public access to industry/destination contingency plans and by a professional attitude towards safety and security aspects.

Source: Tourist Safety and Security: Practical Measures for Destinations. Second edition. World Tourism Organization. 1997.

Figure 36

LINKING SUSTAINABLE TOURISM AND ECOLOGY

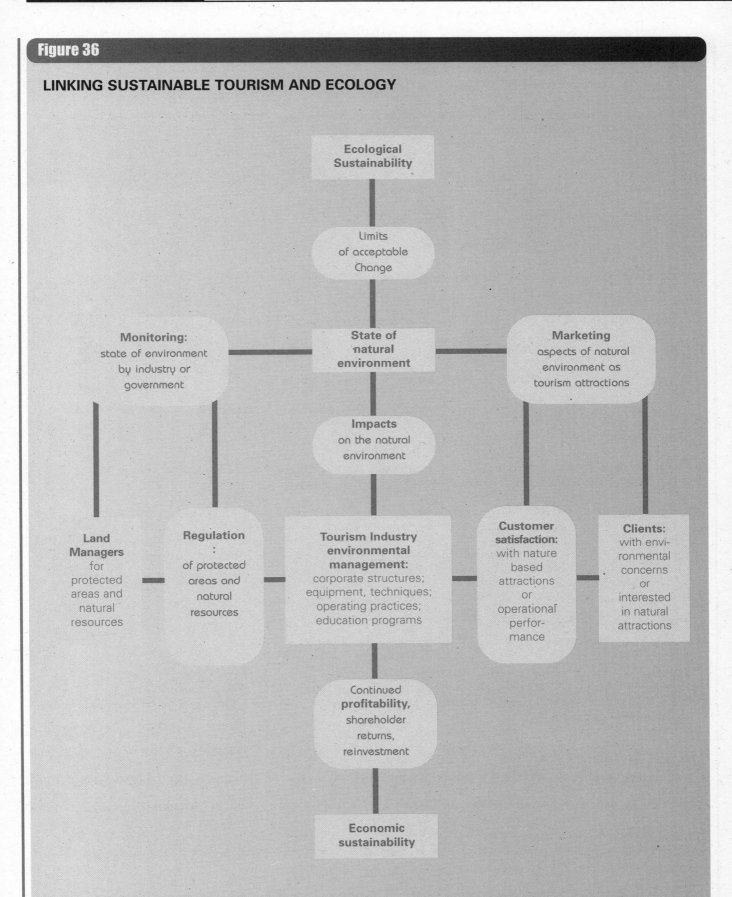

Source: Environmental Guidelines for Coastal Tourism Development in Sri Lanka. 1995. Kate Sullivan, et al. Sri Lanka: Coastal Resources Management Project.

Figure 37

ROLES IN SUPPORTING RESPONSIBLE TOURISM: A CHECKLIST

This checklist describes what can be done to support sustainable tourism by government, non-governmental organizations (NGOs), the tourism industry and individual tourists.

What can government do?

- Government can incorporate sustainable tourism development in the planning process by:

- Working with inter-governmental organizations (IGOs),

- Undertaking research into the environmental, cultural, and economic effects,

- Establishing economic models to help define appropriate levels and types of economic activities for natural and urban areas,

- Developing standards and regulations for environmental and cultural impact assessments,

- Monitoring and auditing existing and proposed tourism developments, and

- Implementing regional environmental accounting systems for the tourism industry.

- Government can include tourism in land use planning to minimize conflict with traditional uses of land and ensure that carrying capacities of tourism destinations reflect sustainable levels of development and are monitored and adjusted appropriately.

- Government can develop design and construction standards which will ensure that tourism development projects are sympathetic to local culture and natural environments.

- Government can develop adequate tools and techniques to analyze the effect of tourism development projects on heritage sites and ancient monuments as an integral part of cultural and environmental impact assessment.

- Government can enforce regulations to prevent illegal trade in historic objects and crafts, unofficial archaeological research, erosion of aesthetic values, and desecration of sacred sites.

- Government can create tourism advisory boards that involve indigenous populations, the general public, industry, NGOs, and others, and include all stakeholders in the decision making process.

- Government can promote and support sustainable tourism development by:

- Developing educational and awareness programmes for the public,

- Briefing all governmental departments involved in tourism or any related department such as natural resources, historic preservation, the arts, and others,

- Ensuring that tourism interests are represented at major environmental and economic planning meetings, and

- By including a policy of sustainable tourism development in all national and local tourism development agreements.

What can be done by non-governmental organizations, which represent and protect the interests of the public?

- NGOs can participate in sustainable tourism advisory boards at all levels of government and industry. This could include assessment of regional, as well as site-specific, development plans and the appropriate mix and location of different land use designations.

- NGOs can seek local support for appropriate sustainable tourism development and oppose inappropriate tourism development.

- NGOs can promote the involvement of local residents in sustainable tourism research and data collection.

- NGOs can become involved in educating the public about the economic importance of sustainable tourism development, the need for a secure resource base (particularly natural landscapes), and appropriate behaviour on the part of government, the tourism industry and tourists.

- NGOs can monitor impacts of tourism on the local culture and environment, equity participation in local tourism development, impacts of other sectors of the economy on sustainable tourism, and government and industry commitments to sustainable tourism.

What can be done by the tourism industry, which delivers products and services to the tourist?

- The tourism industry can protect the biosphere; for example, by minimizing and eliminating use of herbicides on golf courses and artificial snow on ski hills, and by supporting parks and reserves at key sites.

- The tourism industry can ensure sustainable use of land, water, and forests in tourism development activities.

- The tourism industry can reduce and dispose appropriately of wastes; for example, by recycling, reusing and reducing wherever possible, and by having high standards for sewage treatment and waste disposal.

- The tourism industry can adopt energy efficiency practices; for example, by maximizing the use of solar power, wind power and other appropriate sources when possible.

- The tourism industry can minimize health risks; for example, by avoiding hazardous locations such as those near malarial swamps, active volcanoes, and nuclear sites.

- The tourism industry can undertake green marketing; for example, by promoting tourism which minimizes adverse environmental and cultural impacts, and by informing and educating tourists about the impacts of their presence.

- The tourism industry can mitigate damage; for example, by replacing or restoring degraded environments and compensating for local adverse effects.

- The tourism industry can provide complete and credible information to tourists.

- The tourism industry can incorporate environmental values into management decisions; for example, by ensuring environmental representation at the executive level on boards and other management groups.

- The tourism industry can conduct regular environmental audits; for example, by conducting independent assessments of environmental performance of the entire business operations including water quality, carrying capacity, energy consumption, environmental aesthetics, and waste disposal.

What can he done by individual tourists, the ultimate users of the environment?

- Individual tourists can choose businesses which have the reputation of ethical and environment responsibility.

- Individual tourists can learn about and respect the human and natural heritage of the host communities, including the geography, history, customs, and current local concerns.

- Individual tourists can travel in a culturally and environmentally sensitive manner, refraining from inappropriate behaviour which negatively affects the host community or degrades the local natural environment.

- Individual tourists can refrain from purchasing or using those products, services and transportation which endanger the local ecology and culture.

- Individual tourists can practice minimal impact travel.

- Individual tourists can support resource conservation activities in the host countries.

Source: Globe '90 Conference, Tourism Stream, Action Strategy for Sustainable Tourism Development. Vancouver, BC, Canada, 1990.

Questions for Discussion

MANAGING TOURISM IN YOUR AREA

1. Does your area or community have a local tourism department and, if so, how is it organised? How could the organisational structure be improved for more effective management? Does it have sufficient budget and staff?

2. Are there any private sector tourism associations organised in your area and, if so, how effective are they? If there are not any existing associations, which ones do you think should be organised?

3. Has a tourism data base or tourism management information system been established for your area? If so, how could it be improved? If a data base is not set up, what types of information should be placed in a future information system?

4. What aspects of tourism in your area at present and in the future do you think should be monitored? How should a monitoring programme in your area be organised?

5. What approaches should be used to maintain the vitality of tourism in your area?

6. Is there any tourism awareness programme underway in your area and how effective is it? What do you believe are the most effective tourism awareness techniques to be applied in your area?

7. Are any tourism subjects included in your area's education system curriculum?

8. What aspects of local customs, cultural patterns and other factors should be included in a tourist behaviour code for your area?

9. What are the important factors of tourist safety and security that should be considered in your area?

10. If any of the tourism sites in your area are likely to reach saturation levels in the foreseeable future, what measures should be applied to prevent this from happening?

11. Is it possible to disperse tourists more throughout your area to relieve congestion on particular tourism sites?

12. Has the local government or tourism department in your area adopted any programme to handle crises when they arise?

13. Identify the respective responsibilities of the government, private sector, NGOs and the tourists in managing tourism development in your area. Figure 37 can be used as a guide in preparing this list.

annexes

annex 1

TOURISM BILL OF RIGHTS AND TOURIST CODE

The General Assembly of the World Tourism Organization at its sixth ordinary session held in Sofia (Peopleís Republic of Bulgaria) from 17 to 26 September 1985:

1. AWARE of the importance of tourism in the life of peoples because of its direct and positive effects on the social , economic, cultural and educational sectors of national society and the contribution it can make, in the spirit of the United Nations Charter and the Manila Declaration on World Tourism, to improving mutual understanding, bringing peoples closer together and, consequently, strengthening international cooperation ,

2. RECALLING that, as recognized by the General Assembly of the United Nations, the World Tourism Organization has a central and decisive role in the development of tourism with a view to contributing, in accordance with Article 3 paragragh 1 of its Statutes, ìto economic development, international understanding, peace, prosperity and universal respect for, and observation of , human rights and fundamental freedoms for all without distinction as to race, sex, language or religionî

3. RECALLING the Universal Declaration of Human Rights adopted by the General Assembly of the United Nations on 10 December 1948, and in particular Article 24 which provides that ìEveryone has the right to rest and leisure, including reasonable limitation of working hours and periodic holidays with payî, as well as the International Covenant on Economic, Social and Cultural Rights adopted by the General Assembly of the United Nations on 16 December 1966, which invites States to ensure for everyone ìRest, leisure and reasonable limitation of working hours and periodic holidays with pay, as well as remuneration for public holidaysî,

4. CONSIDERING the resolution and recommendations adopted by the United Nations Conference on International Travel and Tourism (Rome, September 1963), and particularly those aimed at promoting tourism development in the various countries and at simplifying government formalities in respect of international travel,

5. DRAWING ITS INSPIRATION from the principles set forth in the Manila Declaration on World Tourism adopted by the World Conference on 10 October 1980, which emphasizes the true, human dimension of tourism, recognizes the new role of tourism as an appropriate instrument for improving the quality of life of all peoples and as a vital force for peace and international understanding and defines the responsibility of States for developing tourism and, in particular, for fostering awareness of tourism among the peoples of the world and protecting and enhancing the tourism resources which are part of mankind's heritage, with a view to contributing to the establishment of a new international economic order,

6. SOLEMNLY AFFIRMING, as a natural consequence of the right to work, the fundamental right of everyone, as already sanctioned by the Universal Declaration of Human Rights, to rest, leisure and periodic holidays with pay and to use them for holiday purposes, to travel freely for education and pleasure and to enjoy the advantages of tourism, both within his country of residence and abroad,

7. INVITES the States to draw inspiration from the principles set forth below substituting the Tourism Bill of Rights Code, and to apply them in accordance with the procedures prescribed in the legislation and regulations of their own countries.

TOURISM BILL OF RIGHTS

Article I

1) The right of everyone to rest and leisure, reasonable limitation of working hours, periodic leave with pay and freedom of movement without limitation, within the bounds of law, is universally recognized.

2) The exercise of this right constitutes a factor of social balance and enhancement of national and universal awareness.

Article II

As a consequence of this right, the States should formulate and implement policies aimed at promoting the harmonious development of domestic and international tourism and leisure activities for the benefit of all those taking part in them.

Article III

To this end the States should:

- encourage the orderly and harmonious growth of both domestic and international tourism ;
- integrate their tourism policies with overall development policies at all levels—local, regional, national and international and broaden tourism cooperation within both a bilateral and multilateral framework, including that of the World Tourism Organization;
- give due attention to the principles of the Manila Declaration on World Tourism and the Acapulco Document while formulating and implementing, as appropriate, their tourism policies, plans and programmes, in accordance with their national priorities and within the framework of the programme of work of the World Tourism Organization" *;
- encourage the adoption of measures enabling everyone to participate in domestic and international tourism, especially by a better allocation of work and leisure time, the establishment or improvement of systems of annual leave with pay and the staggering of holiday dates and by particular attention to tourism for the young, elderly and disabled; and
- in the interest of present and future generations, protect the tourism environment which, being at once human, natural, social and cultural, is the legacy of all mankind.

Article IV

The States should also :

- encourage the access of domestic and international tourists to the heritage of the host communities by applying the provisions of existing facilitation instruments issuing from the United Nations, the International Civil Aviation Organization, the International Maritime Organization, the Customs Co-operation Council or from any other body, the World Tourism Organization in particular, with a view to increasingly liberalizing travel;
- promote tourism awareness and facilitate contact between visitors and host communities with a view to their mutual understanding and betterment;
- ensure the safety of visitors and the security of their belongings through preventive and protective measures;
- afford the best possible conditions of hygiene and access to health services as well as of the prevention of communicable diseases and accidents;
- prevent any possibility of using tourism to exploit others for prostitution purposes; and
- reinforce, for the protection of tourists and the population of the host community, measures to prevent the illegal use of narcotics.

Article V

The States should lastly:

- permit domestic and international tourists to move freely about the country, without prejudice to any limitative measures taken in the national interest concerning certain areas of the territory;
- not allow any discriminatory measures in regard to tourists;
- allow tourists prompt access to administrative and legal services and to consular representatives, and make available internal and external public communications; and
- contribute to the information of tourists with a view to fostering understanding of the customs of the populations constituting the host communities at places of transit and sojourn.

Article VI

The populations constituting the host communities in places of transit and sojourn are entitled to free access to their own tourism resources while fostering respect, through their attitude and behaviour, for their natural and cultural environment.

They are also entitled to expect from tourists understanding of and respect for their customs, religions and other elements of their cultures which are part of the human heritage.

To facilitate such understanding and respect, the dissemination of appropriate information should be encouraged on :

- the customs of host communities, their traditional and religious practices, local taboos and sacred sites and shrines which must be respected;
- their artistic, archaelogical and cultural treasures which must be preserved; and
- wildlife and other natural resources which must be protected.

Article VII

The populations constituting the host communities in places of transit and sojourn are invited to receive tourists with the greatest possible hospitality, courtsey and respect necessary for the development of harmonious human and social relations.

Article VIII

Tourism professionals and suppliers of tourism and travel services can make a positive contribution to tourism development and to implementation of the provisions of this Bill of Rights.

They should conform to the principles of this Bill of Rights and honour commitments of any kind entered into within the context of their professional activities, ensuring the provision of quality products so as to help affirm the humanist nature of tourism.

They should in particular refrain from encouraging the use of tourism for all forms of exploitation of others.

Article IX

Encouragement should be given to tourism professionals and suppliers of tourism and travel services by granting them, through appropriate national and international legislation, the necessary facilities to enable them to:
- exercise their activities in favourable conditions, free from any particular impediment or discrimination;
- benefit from general and technical training schemes, both within their countries and abroad, so as to ensure the availability of skilled manpower; and
- cooperate among themselves as well as with the public authorities, through national and international organizations, with a view to improving the coordination of their activities and the quality of their services.

TOURIST CODE

Article X

Tourists should, by their behaviour, foster understanding and friendly relations among peoples, at both the national and international levels, and thus contribute to lasting peace.

Article XI

At places of transit and sojourn tourists must respect the established political, social, moral and religious order and comply with the legislation and regulations in force.

In these places tourists must also:
- show the greatest understanding for the customs, beliefs and behaviour of the host communities and the greatest respect for their natural and cultural heritage;
- refrain from accentuating the economic, social and cultural differences between themselves and the local population;
- be receptive to the culture of the host communities, which is an integral part of the common human heritage;
- refrain from exploiting others for prostitution purposes; and
- refrain from trafficking in, carrying or using narcotics and/or other prohibited drugs.

Article XII

During their travel from one country to another and within the host country tourists should be able, by appropriate government measures, to benefit from:

- relaxation of administrative and financial controls; and
- the best possible conditions of transport and sojourn that can be offered by suppliers of tourism services.

Article XIII

Tourists should be afforded free access, both within and outside their countries, to sites and places of tourist interest and, subject to existing regulations and limitations, freedom of movement in places of transit and sojourn. On access to sites and places of tourist interest and throughout their transit and sojourn, tourists should be able to benefit from:

- objective, precise and complete information on conditions and facilities provided during their travel and sojourn by official tourism bodies and suppliers of tourism services;
- safety of their persons, security of their belongings and protection of their rights as consumers;
- satisfactory public hygiene, particularly so far as accommodation, catering and transport are concerned, information on the effective prevention of communicable diseases and accidents and ready access to health services;
- access to swift and efficient public communications, both internal and external;
- administrative and legal procedures and guarantees necessary for the protection of their rights; and
- the practice of their own religion and the use of existing facilities for that purpose

Article XIV

Everyone is entitled to make his needs known to legislative representatives and public authorities so that he may exercise his right to rest and leisure in order to enjoy the benefits of tourism under the most favourable conditions and, where appropriate and to the extent consistent with law, associate with others for that purpose.

RESOLUTION 38/146 ADOPTED BY THE UNITED NATIONS GENERAL ASSEMBLY AT ITS THIRTY-EIGHTH SESSION ON 19 DECEMBER 1983.

Tourism

Adopted by the General Assembly of the World Tourism Organization at its eleventh session - Cairo (Egypt), 17-22 October 1995 (Resolution A1RES1338 (XI))

Whereas the WTO Tourism Bill of Rights and Tourist Code (Sofia, 1985) calls on States and individuals to prevent any possibility of using tourism to exploit others for prostitution purposes;

Having consulted international and national organizations concerned, both governmental and non-governmental, as well as the representatives of the tourism sector;

Considering the preoccupation of the international community over the persistence of organized sex tourism which, for the purpose of this statement, can be defined as "trips organized from within the tourism sector, or from outside this sector but using its structures and networks, with the primary purpose of effecting a commercial sexual relationship by the tourist with residents at the destination";

Aware of the grave health as well as social and cultural consequences of this activity for both tourist receiving and sending countries, especially when it exploits gender, age, social and economic inequality at the destination visited;

The General Assembly

- Rejects all such activity as exploitative and subversive to the fundamental objectives of tourism in promoting peace, human rights, mutual understanding, respect for all peoples and cultures, and sustainable development;
- Denounces and condemns in particular child sex tourism, considering it a violation of Article 34 of the Convention on the Rights of the Child (United Nations, 1989), and requiring strict legal action by tourist sending and receiving countries;

- Requests governments of both tourist sending and receiving countries to Mobilize their competent departments, including National Tourism Administrations, to undertake measures against organized sex tourism;
- Gather evidence of organized sex tourism and encourage education of concerned government officials and top executives in the tourism sector about the negative consequences of this activity;
- Issue guidelines to the tounism sector insisting that it refrains from organizing any forms of sex tourism, and from exploiting prostitution as a tourist attraction;
- Establish and enforce, where applicable, legal and administrative measures to prevent and eradicate child sex tourism, in particular through bilateral agreements to facilitate, inter alia, the prosecution of tourists engaged in any unlawful sexual activity involving children and juveniles;
- Assist intergovernmental and non-governmental organizations concerned in taking action against organized forms of sex tourism;
- Appeals to donor countries, aid agencies and other sources of finance to engage in tourism development projects seeking to enhance and diversify the supply of tourism services at the destinations affected by sex tourism, so as to foster employment opportunities in the tourism sector, develop its linkages with other sectors of the national economy, and contribute to tourism's social and economic sustainability;
* Commends the tourism companies and tourism industry organizations, as well as non-governmental organizations such as ECPAT, which have already undertaken measures against sex tourism, in particular with respect to the sexual exploitation of children and juveniles;
* Appeals to the travel trade to
  I. Join efforts and cooperate with non-governmental organizations to eliminate organized sex tourism, at both the origin and destination of travel flows, by identifying and focusing on the critical points at which this activity can proliferate;
  2. Educate staff about the negative consequences of sex tourism, including its impact on the image of the tourism sector and tourist destinations, and invite staff to find ways to remove commercial sex services from the tourism offer;
  3. Develop and strengthen professional codes of conduct and industry self-regulatory mechanisms against the practice of sex tourism;

annex

AGENDA 21 ON TRAVEL AND TOURISM

Agenda 21 is a comprehensive programme of action adopted by182 governments at the United Nations Conference on Environment and Development (UNCED), the Earth Summit, on 14 June 1992. The first document of its kind to achieve international consensus, Agenda 21 provides a blueprint for securing the sustainable future of the planet, from now into the twenty-first century. It identifies the environment and development issues which threaten to bring about economic and ecological catastrophe and presents a strategy for transition to more sustainable development practices.

Agenda 21 is a programme of action for Travel & Tourism. The Travel & Tourism industry has a vested interest in protecting the natural and cultural resources which are the core of its business. It also has the means to do so. As the world's largest industry, it has the potential to bring about substantial environmental and socio-economic improvements and to make a significant contribution to the sustainable development of the communities and countries in which it operates. Concerted action from governments and all sectors of the industry will be needed in order to realize this potential and to secure long-term future development.

Agenda 21 defines the role that Travel & Tourism can play in achieving the aims of sustainability. It emphasizes the importance of partnerships between government, industry and other organizations; analyses the strategic and economic importance of Travel & Tourism and demonstrates the enormous benefits in making the whole industry sustainable, rather than simply focusing on "ecotourism".

In its second part, The Agenda presents the programme of action. Chapter 2 addresses government departments with responsibility for Travel & Tourism, national tourism administrations (NTAs) and representative trade organizations. Chapter 3 addresses Travel & Tourism companies. Each chapter presents an overriding aim and a number of priority areas for action. For each priority area, an objective is defined and steps which can be taken to achieve the objective are outlined. Case studies show how organizations around the world are already beginning to tackle some areas.

For government departments, NTAs and representative trade organizations, the overriding aim is to establish systems and procedures to incorporate sustainble development considerations at the core of the decision-making process and to identify actions necessary to bring sustainable tourism development into being. The nine priority areas for action are:

- assessing the capacity of the existing regulatory, economic and voluntary framework to bring about sustainable tourism
- assessing the economic, social, cultural and environmental implications of the organization's operations
- training, education and public awareness
- planning for sustainable tourism development
- facilitating exchange of information, skills and technology relating to sustainable tourism between developed and developing countries
- providing for the participation of all sectors of society
- design of new tourism products with sustainability at their core
- measuring progress in achieving sustainable development
- partnerships for sustainable development

For companies, the main aim is to establish systems and procedures to incorporate sustainable development issues as a part of the core management funtion and to identify actions needed to bring sustainable tourism into being. The ten priority areas for action are:

- waste minimization, reuse and recycling
- energy efficiency, conservation and management

- management of fresh water resources
- waste water management
- hazardous substances
- transport
- land-use planning and management
- involving staff, customers and communities in environmental issues
- design for sustainability
- partnerships for sustainable development

The challenge of achieving the aims laid out in Agenda 21 is not underestimated. It will require fundamental reorientation. However, the costs of inaction will far outweigh those of action. In the short term, damage to the industry's resources will continue and businesses may face increased regulatory or economic penalties particularly in the wake of the United Nations follow-up to the Rio process. In the longer term, Travel & Tourism's future development will depend on the actions taken now in support of Agenda 21.

annex

ESTABLISHING CARRYING CAPACITIES

Establishing tourism carrying capacities is based on the concept of maintaining a level of development and use that will not result in serious environmental deterioration, sociocultural or economic problems, or be perceived by tourists as depreciating their enjoyment and appreciation of the area or tourism site. Carrying capacity analysis is a basic technique being widely applied in tourism and recreation planning (and also wildlife management) to help achieve sustainable development by systematically determining the upper limits of development and visitor use, and optimum use of tourism resources. Any type of development results in some environmental changes. Carrying capacity analysis typically is based on not exceeding the levels of acceptable change. Numerous tourism areas in the world show evidence of having exceeded their carrying capacities. This has resulted in environmental, social and sometimes economic problems, with a decrease in tourist satisfaction and consequent loss of deterioration of tourist markets.

In practice, determining carrying capacities is often not easy or precise, depending on the factors involved. It is based on the assumptions that are made and perceptions of the levels of acceptable change. Carrying capacities may also change through time and can be increased by taking certain actions. However, it remains a very useful technique in guiding planning for sustainable tourism.

Carrying capacities can be established for both undeveloped tourism areas and those that already have some development, and perhaps even reaching or exceeding their saturation levels. It is often the more developed destinations which have become concerned about their capacity levels. Carrying capacities can best be calculated for specific development sites and small tourism areas. At the national, regional and larger tourism area levels, they must be considered more generally. Often at an area-wide level, capacities are based on a total of the capacities of individual sites such as major tourist attractions or resorts.

The measurement criteria presented here are for establishing carrying capacities primarily for tourist destinations. The capacities of the transportation facilities and services used by tourists travelling to their destinations are also important to analyse. Each area and its type of tourism are unique and development objectives will vary from one place to another, especially with respect to local concepts of what are acceptable levels of change to the physical and sociocultural environment. Also the types of tourist markets affect measurement levels. However, some common criteria exist for virtually all places. Some criteria can be evaluated quantitatively while others must be evaluated qualitatively. In determining capacities, the major factors to be considered are described in the following sections.

The Indigenous Physical and Socio-economic Environment

This refers to the capacity of development and visitor use that can be achieved without resulting in damage to the physical (natural and man-made) environment and generating sociocultural and economic problems to the local community, while still benefiting the community and maintaining a proper balance between development and conservation. Exceeding saturation levels will lead to permanent damage to the physical environment or socio-economic problems, or both. The criteria for determining optimum capacities include:

Physical
- acceptable levels of visual impact and congestion
- point at which ecological systems are maintained before damage occurs
- level of tourism that helps conserve wildlife and natural vegetation of both the land and marine environments without degradation

- level of tourism that helps conserve archaeological, historic and cultural monuments without degradation
- acceptable levels of air, water and noise pollution

Economic
- extent of tourism that provides optimum overall economic benefits without economic distortions or inflation
- amount of economic benefits accruing to local communities
- level of tourism employment suited to the human resources of the local communities

Socio-cultural
- extent of tourism development that can be absorbed socially without detriment to the life styles and activities of the local communities
- level of tourism that helps conserve and revitalise, where desirable, arts, crafts, belief systems, ceremonies, customs and traditions
- level of tourism that will not be resented by local residents or pre-empt their use of attractions and amenity features

Infrastructure
- adequate availability of transportation facilities and services
- adequate availability of utility facilities and services of water supply, electric power, waste management of sewage and solid waste collection, treatment and disposal and telecommunications
- adequate availability of other community facilities and services such as those related to public health and safety, and of housing and community services for employees in tourism

The Tourism Image and Product

This refers to the levels of development and number of tourists that are compatible with the image of the tourist destination and tourism product, and the types of experiences that visitors are seeking. If the area exceeds saturation levels, the environment and attractions which visitors have come to experience will be destroyed or degraded. Tourist satisfaction will decrease, and the destination will decline in quality and popularity with a loss or deterioration of the tourist markets. The criteria for determining optimum capacities include:

Physical
- overall cleanliness and lack of pollution of the destination
- lack of undue congestion of the destination including its attractions
- attractiveness of the landscape or townscape including quality and character of architectural design
- conservation and maintenance of ecological systems, flora and fauna of the natural attraction features
- conservation and maintenance of archaeological, historic and cultural monuments

Economic
- cost of the holiday and 'value for money'

Socio-cultural
- intrinsic interest of the indigenous community and its cultural patterns
- quality of the local arts, crafts, cultural performances and cuisine
- friendliness of residents

Infrastructure
- acceptable standards of transportation facilities and services
- acceptable standards of utility services
- acceptable standards of other facilities and services

For each of the criteria, measurement standards must be decided for each particular area. For example, a measurement standard for the amount of sandy beach area and frontage for each tourist staying at a beach resort can be established based on various assumptions of what is acceptable environmentally and necessary to maintain tourist satisfaction.

Seasonality is a major consideration in the concept of carrying capacity. The saturation level of tourist use of a destination is often reached during the peak periods of use, and not during the low season or on an average annual basis. Therefore, carrying capacity must be calculated for the peak period of use. As was reviewed in the text, approaches can be applied to reduce use during the peak period and even out seasonality during the year. This achieves more optimum use of attractions, facilities, services and infrastructure. As was emphasised in the text, for some types of natural attraction features, visitor use may need to be carefully managed, sometimes controlled with respect to establishing maximum numbers of visitors, or prohibited during an ecologically critical period, such as animal breeding seasons.

Source: World Tourism Organization

annex 4

MODEL MUNICIPAL TOURISM POLICY

This model is an example of Municipal Tourism Policy statute. It is intended as a guide or pattern for those wishing to develop, enact or amend a Municipal Tourism Policy statement, regulation or act. This document is for illustrative purposes only and does not represent a best or only approach to developing a Municipal Tourism Policy. (United States Travel and Tourism Administration, of Commerce, Washington, D.C.)

AN ORDINANCE TO ESTABLISH A MUNICIPAL TOURISM POLICY

Be it enacted by the Council of the Municipality of _____

Section I. FINDINGS.
The Council finds that:
1) the City of _____ is endowed with scenic beauty, historical sites, cultural resources and population whose diversity and traditions are attractive to visitors:
2) these resources should be preserved and nurtured, not only because they are appreciated by other Americans and by visitors from other lands, but because they are valued by the City's own residents;
3) tourism contributes to the City's economic well-being by creating jobs and generating income for local businesses;
4) tourism is an educational medium which helps visitors and residents alike to learn about the City's history, natural and cultural resources, and industrial achievements;
5) tourism instills local pride and creates a sense of common interest between local residents and their visitors;
6) the development and promotion of tourism to _____ is in the public interest;
7) tourism to _____ should develop in an orderly manner in order to provide the maximum benefit to the city and its residents;
8) a comprehensive municipal tourism policy is essential if tourism is to grow in an orderly way.

Section II. POLICY
The policy of the City of _____ shall be to:
1) encourage the orderly growth and development of tourism to the city;
2) instill a sense of history in the City's young people by promoting the preservation and restoration of local historic sites, trails, buildings and districts;
3) promote tourism in a manner that will foster visitor understanding and respect for the values, customs, ethnic traditions, and religious beliefs of the people who live here;
4) monitor tourist impact on the basic human rights of local residents and ensure equal access by visitors and residents to public recreation areas;
5) ensure the protection of natural resources and the preservation of geological, archaeological and cultural treasures in tourist areas;
6) promote the city's commercial interests by encouraging the organization of festivals, fairs and craft demonstrations so that visitors may learn about local products and industrial achievements;
7) provide visitors to the city with a hospitable reception;
8) ensure the safety of visitors, the security of their belongings, and the protection of their rights as consumers;
9) afford visitors and residents the best possible conditions of public sanitation:

10) provide every visitor with prompt access to judicial procedures and guarantees necessary to protect his or her rights;

11) facilitate tourism to the City by developing essential infrastructure; providing investment incentives; and requiring Municipal officials to plan for tourist needs and capitalize on local tourism resources;

12) instill a better understanding among the city's residents and civil servants of the importance of tourism to the local economy;

13) ensure that the tourism interest of the city is fully considered by local agencies in their deliberations; and harmonize, to the maximum extent possible, all city activities in support of tourism with the needs of the general public, the political subdivisions of the City and the local tourism industry;

Section III. DUTIES AND RESPONSIBILITIES OF THE MAYOR

The mayor shall be responsible for implementing these policies:

To assist the Mayor in the execution of these responsibilities for tourism, there is established a municipal Office of Tourism headed by a Tourism Coordinator who shall act as the Mayor's special representative to, and ombudsman for, the tourism industry.

The office of Tourism shall, in conjunction with local public and private sector organizations:

1) encourage the development of the City's tourism infrastructure, facilities, services and attractions;

2) encourage the School Board to create opportunities for professional education and training in tourism-related vocations;

3) encourage cooperation between city agencies and private individuals and organizations to advance the city's tourism interests and seek the views of these agencies and the private sector on city tourism programs and policies;

4) develop a comprehensive plan to promote tourism to the City from other cities, states and foreign countries;

5) measure and forecast tourist volume, receipts and impact, both social and economic;

6) give leadership to all concerned with tourism in the city; and

7) perform other functions necessary to the orderly growth and development of tourism;

The Office of Tourism shall assist the Mayor and the Tourism Policy Council, established in Section IV of this Ordinance, to ensure that the municipal tourism interest receives full and fair consideration in the deliberations of the planning and zoning boards, the board of public works, the school board, the street department and the City Council. It shall identify all local agencies whose policies and programs have a significant effect on the local travel industry, monitor those policies and programs, notify the appropriate agencies of the effects of their actions on travel to the city and, if necessary, recommend program or policy modifications.

The Office of Tourism shall encourage the travel industry to accurately portray the city's character and image and to emphasize the city's historic and cultural legacy.

The Office of Tourism shall encourage the development of informational materials for visitors which, among other things, shall:

1) describe the city's history, economy, political institutions, cultural resources, outdoor recreation facilities and principal festivals;

2) urge visitors to protect endangered species, natural resources, archaeological artifacts and cultural treasures;

3) instill the ethic of stewardship of the City's natural resources.

The Office of Tourism shall foster an understanding among City residents and civil servants of the economic importance of hospitality and tourism to the City.

The Office of Tourism shall work with local businesses, including banks and hotels, educational institutions, the State Tourism Division and the United States Travel and Tourism Administration to ensure availability of special services for international visitors, such as currency exchange facilities.

The Office of Tourism shall encourage the reduction of architectural and other barriers which impede travel by physical handicapped persons.

The Department of Public Health or equivalent is charged with ensuring that lakes and streams on local public lands are free of pollutants and are safe for tourist and recreational uses by residents and visitors. With the Office of Tourism and other appropriate agencies, the Department shall take necessary measures, including the development of public information materials, to enlist visitor cooperation in city efforts to protect wildlife and natural resources from overuse and destruction.

The Department shall also enforce standards of sanitation at tourist rest stops and in city parks, lodges, restaurants and other facilities operated for the traveler by the city of its concessionaires. The Street Department shall keep City streets and bridges maintained in order to facilitate tourism to the City.

The Department of Economic Development (or equivalent) is directed to cooperate with appropriate federal, regional, state and local agencies to develop the City's tourism infrastructure. The Department shall work with the state historic preservation office, the Office of Tourism and appropriate federal, state and local agencies, to preserve and restore historic sites with tourist appeal.

Municipal police and other City employees shall receive visitors with courtesy and hospitality.

The Board of Education shall encourage programs to improve career preparation in tourism and upgrade the quality of service by hospitality employees. In public schools, tourism training should be available on the same basis as for other industries, such as agriculture and the building trades.

The Department of Licences and Permits shall establish strict but reasonable standards for the licensing of all cab drivers, charter boat operators and concessionaires.

Section IV. TOURISM POLICY COUNCIL

There is established an inter-agency coordinating council known as the Tourism Policy Council. The Council shall consist of the Mayor, who shall serve as Chairperson; the Tourism Coordinator, and the heads of such other departments as may be appropriate, including, but not limited to, the Department of Public Health, the Department of Parks and Recreations, the Board of Education, the Department of Planning or Economic Development, the Department of Transportation, the Department of Public Works, the Zoning Board and the Police Department.

Each member may designate an alternate to attend sessions of the Council when the member is unable, however, the alternate must be of sufficient rank to be authorized to make decisions committing his/her agency.

The Council shall function as a review panel which shall:

1) consider assessments prepared by the Office of Tourism on the impact of proposed and existing ordinances and regulations on tourism to the city;
2) seek to reduce or eliminate any adverse impacts; and
3) implement the tourism policy described inn Section 11 of this Ordinance

The Vice Chairperson of the Council shall be designated by the Mayor from among the members of the Council. The Chairperson may establish committees of the Council. The committees may include:

1) a legislative review committee to (a)identify proposed and existing City ordinances which may impede the development of tourism or tourism infrastructure; and (b) recommend and prepare such ordinances or amendments as may be necessary to promote orderly tourism growth;
2) a regulatory review committee to (a) identify city regulations that impede tourism; and (b) recommend and prepare for submission to the full Council amendments to promote orderly tourism growth;
3) committees shall meet at the call of their respective chairpersons, who shall be appointed by the Chairpersons of the Council. Committee chairpersons shall serve a term of one year and are eligible for appointment.

The Council and its committees shall be empowered to conduct public hearings and to consult with the travel industry.

Section V. TOURISM ADVISORY BOARD

The Mayor shall appoint a (number)- member Tourism Policy Advisory Board. The members of the Board shall be selected to represent the various components of the local tourism industry. The Board shall advise in developing tourism marketing policies and coordinating City tourism programs with area promotional organizations and the private sector.

Members of the Tourism Advisory Board shall serve without salary for terms established by the Mayor. They shall select from among their number a chairperson and a vice chairperson. Members may be removed for cause and shall be required to refrain from offering advice on any matter involving a project in which they have a direct financial interest.

Section VI. This ordinance shall take effect upon its adoption by the City Council and its approval by the Mayor.

annex 5

CHECKLIST FOR DEVELOPMENT OF ECOTOURISM FACILITIES

The following generalised criteria are suggested as a guideline for preparing more detailed standards related to specific local issues and the ecological characteristics of a given site. With some exceptions, the criteria and the principles they embody may also be applied to other types of development. These are intended as a general guide only and should not be considered a complete list of criteria or as a substitute for professional services.

Site Planning Issues

- Site buildings and structures to avoid cutting significant trees and to minimise disruption of other natural features.
- Use naturally-felled trees whenever possible (such as trees felled by high winds or other natural causes).
- Trail systems should respect travel patterns and habitats of wildlife.
- Erosion control should be considered in all buildings/trail placement.
- Divert water off trails and roads before it gains sufficient flow and velocity to create significant erosion problems.
- Shorelines and beach fronts should not be intensively cleared of vegetation.
- Minimise trail crossing points at rivers and streams.
- Maintain vegetation areas adjacent to lakes, ponds, perennial streams, and intermittent streams as filter strips to minimise runoff of sediment and debris.
- Buildings should be spaced to allow for wildlife travel patterns and forest growth.
- Provide trail head signs to enhance appreciation of the natural environment and to clearly establish rules of conduct. Provide additional rules posted in guest units.
- Discretely label plant/tree types around the immediate lodging facilities to acquaint visitors with species they may encounter in the surrounding preserved/protected areas.
- Utilise low impact site development techniques, such as boardwalks, instead of paved or unpaved trails wherever possible.
- Pastures and corrals for horses and other grazing stock should be located so as not to pollute water sources or watersheds.
- Review any potential sources of sound or smell associated with development that may be disruptive to the environment or offensive to the visitor.
- Design should reflect seasonal variations such as rainy seasons and solar angles.
- Site lighting should be limited and controlled to avoid disruption of wildlife diurnal cycles.

Special care should be taken in planning of trails through untouched areas. It is prudent to hire a naturalist to help place the trail system to minimise disruption of wildlife and plant biosystems. Special attention should be granted to creatures that rely on trees as aerial pathways or habitat. Careful consideration should be taken in the placement of access roads into a site. Vehicular travel within protected areas should be limited if not avoided completely. A civil engineer should also be involved in the design of trails where erosion control may be an issue. Opportunities for handicapped individuals should be provided wherever possible.

Building Design Issues

- Design of buildings should utilise local construction techniques, materials, and cultural images wherever that approach is environmentally sound.
- Provide building forms and images in harmony with the natural environment. Design buildings on long-term environmental standards and not necessarily on short-term material standards.
- Maintenance of ecosystems should take priority over view or dramatic design statements.
- Provide facilities to accommodate messy activities. Placement of boot scrapers, outdoor showers, etc., become a necessity for operation in some areas.

- Consider use of canopies to cover high use trails between structures to minimise erosion and to provide shelter during the rainy season.
- Provide an architecture consistent with environmental philosophies and/or scientific purposes. Avoid contradictions.
- Provide adequate storage for travel gear, such as backpacks, boots, and other camping equipment.
- Use low tech design solutions wherever possible.
- Prominently post an environmental code of conduct for visitors and staff.
- Provide ecotourists with on-site reference materials for environmental studies.
- Interior furnishing and equipment should represent local resources except where special purpose furnishings or equipment are not readily available for local sources.
- Facilities should take advantage of local materials, local craftsmen, and artists wherever possible.
- Use of energy intensive products or hazardous material should be avoided.
- Building practices should respect local cultural standards and morals. Involvement of local inhabitants should be encouraged to provide input for the designer as well as a sense of ownership and acceptance by local residents.
- Hand excavate footings wherever possible.
- Special design consideration should be given to insect, reptile, and rodent control. The sensitive approach to design should minimise opportunities for intrusion rather than the killing of pests.
- Facilities for handicapped individuals should be provided where practical. It is noted, however, that the rugged nature of most ecotourism or scientific sites preclude access for some disabled individuals. Educational facilities should make equal access for the handicapped a strong priority.
- Plan for future growth of the facility to minimise future demolition and waste.
- Construction specifications should reflect environmental concerns regarding use of wood products and other building materials. Refer to "First Cut: A Primer on Tropical Wood Use and Conservation" prepared by the Rainforest Alliance.
- Seismic design considerations should also be taken into account.

Energy Resource and Utility Infrastructure Issues

- Landscape elements should be placed to enhance natural ventilation of the facilities and avoid unnecessary consumption of energy.
- Consider use of passive or active solar or wind energy sources wherever practical.
- Water lines should be located to minimise disruption of earth, adjacent to trails wherever possible.
- Hydroelectric power generation techniques should be utilised with a minimal disruption to the environment.
- Limit use of air conditioning to areas where humidity and temperature control is necessary, such as computer rooms in research facilities. The design approach should utilise natural ventilation techniques to provide for human comfort wherever possible.

Waste Management Issues

- Provide ecologically sound restroom and trash disposal facilities at trail heads for guest and non-guest use.
- Pastures and corrals for horses and other grazing stock should be located so as not to pollute water sources or watersheds.
- Provide for environmentally sound methods of trash removal.
- Provide trash storage secure from animals and insects.
- Provide facilities for recycling.
- Utilise appropriate technologies for the treatment of organic wastes such as composting, septic tanks, or biogas tanks.
- Look at methods to recycle wastewater for non-potable uses and to treat tainted waters before their return to the natural environment.

Source: Ecotourism: A Guide for Planners & Managers. Kreg Lindberg and Donald E. Hawkins, ed. North Bennington, VT, USA: The Ecotourism Society.

annex 6

THE ENVIRONMENTALLY ORIENTED TOUR OPERATOR— RECOMMENDATIONS AND PROPOSALS FOR TOUR OPERATORS

THE TOUR OPERATOR AS A BUSINESS UNDERTAKING

Environmental Management and Information System

1. Enshrinement of binding environmental principles or guidelines for environmentally acceptable and socially responsible tourism and sustainable development as corporate goals.
2. Organisation of environmental responsibilities at the highest level within the company.
3. Systematic surveying of the environmental qualities of the company and of its tourism products.
4. Definition, review and monitoring of environmental standards ("environmental controlling") and development of a comprehensive environmental information system.
5. Evaluation, application/implementation and practical availability of gathered environmental information.
6. Regular compilation of environmental reports by responsible staff/departments on internal areas and products.

Marketing: Product Policy
7. Ecological orientation in product planning and definition of purchasing criteria.

7a. Consideration of environmentally sound management of accommodation and gastronomy enterprises.

Environmental management
- Environmental protection is organised in the enterprise
- There is some form of proof of environmental orientation or environmentally sound management (guidelines, manuals, awards, quality labels, etc.)

The enterprise practises environmentally oriented measures and activities in the fields of:
- Waste: avoidance and management
- Energy: environmentally sound energy supply (for example, use of renewable sources) and reduction of consumption (energy-saving measures)
- Water: reduction of consumption (economy measures) and of pollutant release, environmentally sound effluent disposal (for example, connection to sewage treatment plants), use of rain and non-potable water
- Noise and air: avoidance and abatement of emissions/pollution
- Ecological information for guests on the enterprise and its environment: for example, concerning environmental qualities, any problems or restrictions, suggestions on appropriate and recommended behaviour for holidaymakers, leisure services, information material
- Healthy and environmentally sound catering
- Environmentally sound purchasing, with preference to regional supplies
- Ecologically oriented care and design of outdoor facilities
- Training of staff to behave in an environmentally conscious manner

7b. Consideration of environmentally committed destinations.

Environmental policy

-   A development concept of sustainable tourism development has been presented

. The region practices environmentally oriented measures and activities in the following fields:

-   Monitoring of environmental qualities
-   Planning, construction and operation/use of infrastructure facilities according to environmental aspects (for example, replacement of environmentally damaging facilities by new ones, utilisation or preference of existing environmentally sound structure before creating new ones)
-   Landscape and nature conservation: ecologically oriented construction (such as through planning instruments, architecture), species/habitat conservation
-   Setting up of capacity limits for all infrastructure facilities, such as leisure and sport facilities, heritage attractions and other places of interest, accommodation and gastronomy, transport infrastructure, supply and disposal facilities (waste, energy, water)
-   Determination and designation of zones with specific ecological capacities with regard to buildings and visitors, apply regulatory measures where necessary
-   Transport: promotion of environmentally sound means and modes of transport (such as increased use of bicycles and local public transport, development of environmentally acceptable transport concepts), avoidance or abatement of transport-related pollution
-   Energy: environmentally sound energy supply (such as renewables), reduction of energy consumption, energy conservation
-   Waste: avoidance, disposal (collection, source segregation) and management (recycling, hazardous waste disposal)
-   Water: supply (aspects of potable water capacity and quality), reduction of water consumption (economy measures) and pollutant releases, effluent (wastewater system, treatment and reuse)
-   Bathing waters and beach quality (European Blue Flag award)
-   Noise and air: avoidance and abatement of emissions/pollution, climate protection
-   Information and public relations work: information on environmental qualities, educational campaigns, support programmes, events, production of information material

7c. Low-impact leisure programme.

Sport, excursion and culture programmes

-   Promotion of sports and sporting products and services structured so as to have minimum impacts on nature and environment
-   Performance of environmentally benign sports courses
-   Products and services with ecological focus
-   Control/direction of products and services in ecologically sensitive areas, for example, protected areas
-   Natural phenomena and special attractions of the region
-   'Soft' adventure tours
-   Activity courses (for example, farming, landscape conservation, crafts)

Animation

-   Presentation of environmental aspects at events
-   Inclusion as a matter-of-course component of programmes in such a manner that the issue of 'nature/environment' is easily grasped and positively associated by the holidaymaker
-   Offers of environmental events in which fun, adventure, etc. are in the foreground

7d. Consideration of environmentally sound means and modes of transport.

Environmentally sound arrival and departure

- Promotion of environmentally sound ways of arrival by bicycle, bus, railway and ship wherever possible and reasonable (time needed, quality of connections, distance), particularly for short distances
- Extension of the duration of long-haul journeys, for example as a rule of thumb: number of travelling hours smaller than number of days on holiday
- Promotion of comparable tour offers to nearby distances, for example in the trekking sector
- Increased use of modern, less polluting aircraft
- Clipping transport volume peaks, for example, through using night trains, mid-week arrivals, etc.

Environmentally sound mobility at the destination

- Preferential treatment or promotion of environmentally sound modes of transport (walking, cycling, bus, mountain railway, etc.) and of local public transport in both everyday 'holiday mobility' and in excursion programmes

8. Step-wise increase of the share of environmentally sound tours and services (including accommodation/gastronomy enterprises and transport services) in the overall volume of products and services.

Marketing and Advertising Media: Material and Handling

9. Use of papers and materials with minimum environmental impacts and according to state of the art

10. Suggest or create the structures for distributors to recommend that catalogues are passed on to friends and acquaintances, or are handed back to travel agencies for reuse

11. Reduction of catalogue consumption
- Splitting of the overall catalogue—where products and services are suited to this—into destination and special thematic catalogues, in so far as this reduces the total volume of catalogues per customer
- Use of new media
- Dispatch of catalogues to travel agencies other than those with which regular business relations exist only upon request

12 Participation in and promotion of initiatives of the trade associations for optimised use of catalogues and materials, and for reduction of their consumption.

Marketing: Communication Policy

Catalogues: Contents

13 .Presentation of corporate principles and environmental activities.

14. Environmental information on accommodation, the destination area, transport/traffic situation, leisure/sports, and suggestions for appropriate behaviour of holidaymakers at the locality—perhaps in the form of a matrix.

15. Labelling of accommodation enterprises and destinations that have received environmental awards.

16. Recommendations of particularly ecological products/services

17 .Good and clear placement of environmental information.

18 .Presentation for orientation purposes of typical indexes and pollutant inventories per mode of transport as a function of travelled distance.

Advertising and Public Relations, Information for Guests and Public

19. Aggressive marketing for environmentally benign tour and services.

20. Provision of information for the use of environmentally sound modes of transport and public transport (line maps, timetables, mobility advice)

21. Surveys of and exchange of information with holidaymakers on the ecological 'satisfaction' of their tour

22. Offer to customers to acquire further information upon request on environmental issues at the travel agency.

23. Offer to customers to request environmental information from the tour operator at the destination or accommodation.

24. Handing out of information material (bicycle maps, information brochures) and recommendations for travel guides and literature in the travel agency before and during the booking.

Training

25. Regular environmental training of staff at head office, at least once a year.

26. Regular information and further education of field staff (tour leaders, hotel purchasers, animators, guides) on ecological issues and the local situation (in accommodation and destination in general)

27. Offers of central, joint training of business partners in the industry (for example, accommodation enterprises, travel agencies)

Co-operation

28. Activities at the destination

- Co-ordination with business partners, politicians, municipal bodies and nature and environmental organisations

29. Co-ordination with travel agencies

- Distribution of information on environmental aspects of a tour (for example transport, destinations, accommodation enterprises) and references to further sources of information (media, organisations)
- Support in selling environmentally sound products and services through commission structures or bonus systems
- joint advertising campaigns and actions for environmentally benign travelling

30. Maintenance of contacts and co-operation with nature/environmental organisations.

- Exchange of information on the ecological situation in the destinations
- Joint initiatives such as the dissemination of information and performance of information events, presentations, seminars and guided tours
- Structuring of special tourism and leisure programmes
- Project promotion/sponsoring of actions in the destination area

31. Support of business partners
- Motivation and recommendations to participate in environmental competitions or pioneering projects

32. Co-operation with other tour operators

- Co-operative actions in dealings with common partners such as travel agencies, accommodation enterprises, destinations (surveying of environmental qualities, strategies, monitoring)

33. Co-operation with educational institutions (universities) for the preparation of studies, diploma theses, etc.

Political Activities

34. Participation in the bodies of tourism associations/federations and other bodies with environmental relevance (for example 'round tables', working groups, project partnerships).

35. Support of political lobbying for improvement of regulatory, fiscal and financial framework conditions for environmentally oriented tour operators.

Source: Adapted from The Environmentally Oriented Tour Operator—Recommendations and Proposals for Tour Operators prepared by The Association for Ecological Tourism in Europe with the support of the German Federal Ministry for the Environment.

SUPPLEMENTARY INDICATORS OF SUSTAINABLE TOURISM

In some of the following lists core indicators are also occasionally included. For certain tourism issues, they are especially relevant and, therefore, deserve mention.

Coastal Zones

ISSUE	INDICATORS	SUGGESTED MEASURES
ecological destruction	amount degraded	- % in degraded condition
beach degradation	levels of erosion	- % of beach eroded
fish stocks depletion	reduction in catch	- effort to catch fish
		- fish counts for key species
overcrowding	use intensity *	- persons per metre of accessible beach
disruption of fauna (e.g., whales)	species counts	- number of species
		- change in species mix
		- number of key species sightings
diminished water quality	pollution levels	- fecal coliform and heavy metals counts
lack of safety	crime levels {9}	
	accident levels	- N° of crimes reported (theft, assault)
		- water related accidents as a % of tourist population

Mountains

ISSUE	INDICATORS	SUGGESTED MEASURES
loss of flora and fauna	reproductive success of indicator species continuing presence of wildlife at traditionally occupied sites	- species counts
		- changes in mix of species
		- number of road kills of specified
		- visual inspection and photographic record**
erosion	extent of erosion caused by tourists rate of continuing erosion	- % of surface in eroded state
		- visual inspectionas and photographic record
lack of access to key sites	length of vehicle line-ups	- number of hours spent in vehicle
		- cost of entry/lowest average local wage

lack of solitude	consumer satisfaction *	- number of people at peak period (accessible area only) - questionnaire on whether solitude objectives met
loss of aesthetic qualities	site attraction *	- visibility of human presence (e.g., litter counts)
diminished water quality	pollution counts	- measures of fecal coliform, heavy metal

** Local wildlife/biodiversity management offices may provide long-term records for some species

Managed Wildlife Parks

ISSUE	INDICATORS	SUGGESTED MEASURES
poor species health groups	reproductive rate of key species	- monitoring of numbers for animal
	species diversity change in mix of animal species	- species counts - key species population counts
overcrowding	use intensity *	- number of visitors - ratio of people/game animals (peak period)
human encroachment	human population in park and surrounding area activities of people in park and surrounding area	- number of people within 10km of boundary - % of park area affected by unauthorized human activity (squatting, wood cutting) - % of surrounding land being used for human purposes such as agriculture (10km radius)
poaching reported	level of poaching in park	- number of incidents of poaching - reduction of affected flora and fauna assets
lack of safety	human/animal interaction	- number of human/animal contacts reported involving human injury ** - crimes against tourists

** May be a measure of either more contacts or a change in the level of reporting.

Urban Environments

ISSUE	INDICATORS	SUGGESTED MEASURES
lack of safety	crime levels types of crimes commited traffic safety	- number of crimes reported (e.g., thef and assault)** - traffic injuries as a % ofpopulation
uncleanliness	site attraction*	- counts of levels of waste on site
crowding at key urban attributes	use intensity*	- traffic congestion - length of wait

degradation of key urban attributes	SEE CULTURAL SITES BUILT HERITAGE BELOW	
health threats	air pollution measurements	- air pollution indices (e.g., sulphur dioxide, nitrogen oxide, particulates) - number of days exceedingspecified pollutant standards
	drinking water quality	- availability of clean water (e.g., can tap water be consumed on site)
	type and extent of communicable diseases	- statistics on disease prevalence
	noise levels	- records on decibel count at key locations

** May be a function of change in level of crime or changes in level of reporting

Cultural Sites - Built Heritage

ISSUE	INDICATORS	SUGGESTED MEASURES
site degradation	restoration costs	- estimated costs to maintain/restore site per annum
	levels of pollutants affecting site	- acidity of precipitation
	measures of behaviour disruptive to site	- traffic vibration (ambient level) - number of incidents of vandalism reported
determining tourism capacity	use intensity*	
lack of safety	crime rate and type	- number and type of crimes against tourists reported**

** May be a function of change in level of crime or changes in level of reporting.

Unique Ecological Sites (often ecotourism destinations)

ISSUE	INDICATORS	SUGGESTED MEASURES
ecosystem degradation	number and mix of species continued presence of key species in traditionally occupied areas	- species count - count of members of key species - number of tourist sightings of key
species	reproductive success of key species	- areas of species occupation (flora and fauna)**
	site degradation changes in flora mix and concentration	- primary flora species as a % of total plant cover - number of outfitters/guides using site • number of boats using site • % of area negatively affected

** Local wildlife/biodiversity management offices may provide long-term records for some species.

Cultural Sites (Traditional communities)

ISSUE	INDICATORS	SUGGESTED MEASURES
violation of social and cultural norms	languages spoken by locals	• % of community speaking a non-local language
displacement of members of local population	social impact*	• average met income of tourists/average net income of local population • number of retail establishments/number of establishments serving local needs (as opposed to tourists) • % of local establishments open year-round
	local satisfaction*	• number and type of complaints by locals**

** May be a function of change in number of incidents or changes in level of reporting.

Small Islands

ISSUE	INDICATORS	SUGGESTED MEASURES
currency leakage	measures of capital flight	• % of exchange leakage from total tourism revenues
high levels of foreign ownership	value of foreign ownership	• % of foreign ownership of tourism establishments
lack of jobs for local population	local jobs created through tourism	• % of jobs supported by tourism • % of seasonal jobs
fresh water shortage	fresh water availability	• volume of water used by tourists/volume used by local population on per capita basis • cost to supply water • cost to supply water/# of tourists • estimates of capacity (e.g., vol remaining in reservoir/aquifer)
electricity shortage	electricity availability	• # of brown outs • restrictions on use • changes in cost for electricity use
sewage disposal	sewage treatment facilities	• volume of sewage treated/total volume of sewage • level of treatment

SEE COASTAL ZONE CATEGORY
FOR INDICATORS ASSOCIATED
WITH BEACH DEGRADATION

annex 8

RESOLUTION FROM THE EXPERTS MEETING ON TOURIST SAFETY AND SECURITY
World Tourism Organization, Madrid, Spain, 11-12 April 1994

Recalling the Manila Declaration on World Tourism (1980) which affirmed that tourism is an activity essential to the life of nations and that its development is linked to the freedom of travel,

Recalling further World Tourism Organization resolution A/RES/317(X) adopted by the General Assembly at its tenth session (Bali, Indonesia, October 1993)*,

We, the experts, believe that the ability of citizens of all countries to travel in safety is a fundamental human right,

We welcome the efforts being made by countries, organisations and other entities to develop and strengthen medical services as well as the operation of the criminal justice system. Such efforts not only promote the well-being of the general public, but support travel and tourism as an important component of the economy of entire regions and countries and a powerful generator of jobs.

We condemn all attacks and threats which undermine this basic right to travel, and express our support for all countries and individuals who are suffering from crime and terrorism directed against travellers and tourists.

We recommend that member States of the World Tourism Organization and all other organisations concerned with travel and tourism adopt as a matter of urgency the following practical measures to promote the safety and security of travellers and tourists:

1. The gathering of comprehensive statistics and research that result in reliable information and data suitable for intelligent risk assessment by decision-makers and policy-makers.

2. The establishment of local, national and international clearing-houses of model programmes and good practices in tourist safety and security for use as a resource base by governments, the travel industry and individuals.

3. The training and education of travel employees and private and public sector service personnel in their role as guardians responsible for protecting the basic right of safe travel by all citizens of the world.

4. The development of private sector/public sector partnerships in the facilitation of safety-conscious travel and in ensuring the growth of the national economy.

5. The implementation of programmes of emergency services for travellers and tourists in need in order to assist them and, in the event of crime, to permit the successful prosecution of offenders at the least possible burden to the victims.

6. The allocation of adequate resources to the courts, the police and public and private security forces for the protection and general well-being of travellers and tourists.

7. The development of national legislation to address the security and protection of travellers and tourists.
* A/RES/317(X): Security and protection of tourists (agenda item 12):

The General Assembly,

Recalling its resolution on the security and protection of tourists (A/RES/177(VI) adopted in 1985,

Noting that violence and criminal acts against travellers, tourists and tourism facilities are a global problem,

1.   Condemns all violence, threat of violence and all criminal acts against travellers, tourists and tourism facilities,

2.   Calls on States to take all appropriate measures against those who perpetrate such criminal acts and to safeguard travellers, tourists and tourism facilities against any form of violence or criminal activity, and

3.   Requests the Secretary-General to develop practical measures that countries might employ to deal with violence and criminal acts against travellers, tourists and tourism facilities.

Source: Tourist Safety and Security. 1996. Madrid: World Tourism Organization.

bibliography

Ashworth, G. J. and J. E. Tunbridge. 1990. *The Tourist-Historic City*. London and New York: Belhaven Press.

Boniface, Priscilla and Peter J. Fowler. 1993. *Heritage and Tourism in 'The Global Village'*. London and New York: Routledge.

Boo, Elizabeth. 1990. Ecotourism: *The Potentials and Pitfalls*, Volumes 1 and 2. Washington, DC: World Wildlife Fund.

Ceballos-Lascurain, Hector. 1996. *Tourism, Ecotourism and Protected Areas*. Cambridge, UK: International Union for Conservation of Nature and Natural Resources (IUCN).

Cooper, Chris, et al. 1993. *Tourism: Principles and Practices*. London: Pitman Publishing.

Doswell, Roger. 1997. Tourism: *How Effective Management Makes the Difference*. Oxford, UK: Butterworth-Heinemann.

Edington, John M. and M. Ann Edington. 1986. *Ecology, Recreation and Tourism*. Cambridge, UK: Cambridge University Press.

Gee, Chuck Y. , et al. 1997. *The Travel Industry*. Third edition. New York: Van Nostrand Reinhold.

Getz, Donald. 1991. *Festivals, Special Events, and Tourism*. New York: Van Nostrand Reinhold.

Gunn, Clare A. 1994. *Tourism Planning: Basics, Concepts, Cases*. Third Edition. Washington, DC: Taylor & Francis.

— 1997. *Vacationscape: Developing Tourist Areas*. Third Edition. Washington, DC: Taylor & Francis.

Harrison, Lynn C. and Winston Husbands. 1996. *Practising Responsible Tourism: International Case Studies in Tourism Planning, Policy and Development*. New York: John Wiley & Sons, Sons.

Hawkins, Donald E. et al, eds. 1995. *The Ecolodge Sourcebook for Planners & Developers*. North Bennington, VT, USA: The Ecotourism Society.

Hetherington, Arlene. 1991. *Rural Tourism: Marketing Small Communities*. Meta-Link, USA.

Inskeep, Edward. 1991. *Tourism Planning: An Integrated and Sustainable Development Approach*. New York: Van Nostrand Reinhold.

Kadt, Emanuel de, ed. 1979. *Tourism: Passport to Development?* A Joint World Bank-UNESCO publication. Oxford, UK: Oxford University Press.

Kotler, Donald H. et al. 1993. *Marketing Places*. New York: The Free Press.

Kuss, Fred R. et al. 1990. *Visitor Impact Management*. Vols. 1 and 2. Washington, DC: National Parks and Conservation Association.

Lawson, Fred. 1995. *Hotels and Resorts: Planning, Design and Refurbishment*. Oxford, UK: Butterworth-Heinemann.

Lea, John. 1988. *Tourism and Development in the Third World*. London and New York: Routledge.

Lickorish, Leonard J. et al. 1991. *Developing Tourism Destinations*. Harlow, Essex, UK.

Lindberg, Kreg. 1991. *Policies for Maximizing Nature Tourism's Ecological and Economic Benefits*. Washington, DC: World Resources Institute.

Lindberg, Kreg & Donald E. Hawkins. 1993. *Ecotourism: A Guide for Planners & Managers*. North Bennington, VT, USA: The Ecotourism Society.

Lindberg, Kreg, et al. eds. 1998. *Ecotourism : A Guide for Planners and Managers*, Volume II. North Bennington, VT, USA: The Ecotourism Society.

McHarg, Ian L. 1991. *Design with Nature*. New York: John Wiley & Sons.

McIntosh, Robert W. and Charles R. Goeldner. 1994. *Tourism: Principles, Practices and Philosophies*. Seventh edition. New York: John Wiley & Sons.

Mertes, James D. and James R. Hall. 1995. *Park, Recreation, Open Space and Greenway Guidelines*. Washington, DC: National Recreation and Park Association.

Middleton, Victor T. C. 1994. *Marketing in Travel and Tourism*. Oxford: Heinemann.

Mill, Robert Christie and Alastair M. Morrison. 1997. Third edition. *The Tourism System: An Introductory Text*. Englewood Cliffs, NJ, USA: Prentice-Hall.

Morrison, Alastair M. 1996. *Hospitality and Travel Marketing*. London: Chapman & Hall.

Murphy, Peter E. 1985. *Tourism: A Community Approach*. New York and London: Methuen.

National Parks and Conservation Association. 1990. *Visitor Impact Management*. Volumes One and Two. Washington, DC.

National Trust for Historic Preservation in the United States. 1993. *Getting Started: How to Succeed in Heritage Tourism*. Washington, DC.

National Trust for Historic Preservation and National Tour Association. 1995. *Touring Historic Places: A Manual for Group Tour Operators and Managers of Historic and Cultural Attractions*. Washington, DC.

Overseas Development Administration. 1988. *Appraisal of Projects in Developing Countries: A Guide for Economists*. London: HMSO.

Pearce, Douglas. *Tourist Development*. 1996. Third edition. Harlow, Essex, UK: Longman Scientific & Technical.

Pearce, Philip L., et al. 1996. *Tourism Community Relationships*. Oxford, UK: Pergamon..

Petersen, David C. 1996. *Sports, Convention, and Entertainment Facilities*. Washington, DC: Urban Land Institute.

Rapaport, Dave. ed. no date. *Creating Environmentally Sound Resorts*. Suva, Fiji: Greenpeace Pacific.

Rogers, Adam. 1993. *The Earth Summit: A Planetary Reckoning*. Los Angeles: Global View Press.

Schwanke, Dean, et al. 1997. *Resort Development Handbook*. Washington, DC: Urban Land Institute.

Singh Tej Vir, et al. 1989. *Towards Appropriate Tourism: The Case of Developing Countries*. Frankfurt am Mein: Peter Lang.

Smith, Stephen L. J. 1995. *Tourism Analysis: A Handbook*. Second edition. Harlow, Essex, UK.

Smith, Valene L. ed. 1989. *Hosts and Guests: The Anthropology of Tourism*. second edition. Philadelphia: University of Pennsylvania Press.

Smith, Valene L. and William R. Eadington. ed. 1992. *Tourism Alternatives: Potentials and Problems in the Development of Tourism*. Philadelphia: University of Pennsylvania.

Sullivan, Kate, et al. ed. 1995. *Environmental Guidelines for Coastal Tourism Development in Sri Lanka*. Sri Lanka: Coastal Resources Management Project.

The Ecotourism Society. 1993. *Ecotourism Guidelines for Nature Tour Operators*. North Bennington, VT, USA.
— Responsible Travel Guidelines Collection.1995. North Bennington, VT, USA.

The Ecotourism Society. 1995. *Marine Ecotourism Information Package*. North Bennington, VT, USA.
United States National Park Service (United States Department of the Interior). 1993. Guiding Principles of Sustainable Design. Denver Service Center.

University of Missouri, Department of Recreation and Park Administration. 1986. *Guidelines for Tourism Development*. Prepared for the US Department of Commerce, Travel and Tourism Administration and Economic Development Administration. USA.

Weiler, Betty and Collin Michael Hall. 1992. *Special Interest Tourism*. London: Belhaven Press.

Whelan, Tensie, ed. 1991. *Nature Tourism: Managing for the Environment*. Washington, DC: Island Press.

Witt, Stephen F. and Luiz Moutinho. Ed. 1995. Second edition. *Tourism Marketing and Management Handbook*. New York: Prentice Hall.

Witt, Stephen F., et al. 1992. *The Management of International Tourism*. London and New York: Routledge.

World Commission on Environment and Development. 1987. *Our Common Future*. Oxford, UK: Oxford University Press.

World Tourism Organization Publications (available from WTO in Madrid)

World Tourism Organization and World Health Organisation. 1991. *Regional Conference for Africa and the Mediterranean on Food Safety and Tourism*. Tunis, Tunisia.

World Tourism Organization and United Nations Environment Programme. 1992. *Guidelines: Development of National Parks and Protected Areas for Tourism*. Madrid.

World Tourism Organization, United Nations Environment Programme and Foundation for Environmental Education in Europe. 1996. *Awards for Improving the Coastal Environment: The Example of the Blue Flag*.

World Tourism Organization, World Travel and Tourism Council, The Earth Council. 1995. *Agenda 21 for the Travel and Tourism Industry: Towards Environmentally Sustainable Development.*

World Tourism Organization and European Tourism Action Group. 1996. *Joint Seminar on Tourism and Environmental Protection.* Heidelberg, Germany.

World Tourism Organization and Department of Tourism, Philippines. 1997. *World Tourism Leaders' Meeting on The Social Impacts of Tourism.* Manila, Philippines.

World Tourism Organization. 1991. *Seminar on New Forms of Demand and New Products.* Nicosia, Cyprus.

— 1992. *An Integrated Approach to Resort Development.* Madrid, Spain.

— 1993. *Seminar on Tourism Development and the Responsibility of the State.* Budapest, Hungary.

— 1994. *National and Regional Tourism Planning: Methodologies and Case Studies.* London and New York: Routledge.

— 1994. *Seminar on Quality -A Challenge for Tourism.* . Madrid.

— 1996. *Seminar on Rural Tourism: A Solution for Employment, Local Development and Environment.* Hotel Shefayim Kibbutz, Israel.

— 1996. *Directory of Multilateral and Bilateral Sources of Financing for Tourism Development.* Madrid.

— 1996. *Tourist Safety and Security: Practical Measures for Destinations.* Madrid.

— 1996. *What Tourism Managers Need to Know: A Practical Guide to the Development and Use of Indicators of Sustainable Tourism.* Madrid.

— 1996. *Towards New Forms of Public-Private Sector Partnership: The Changing Role, Structure and Activities of National Tourism Administrations.* Madrid.

— 1997. *WTO Silk Road Forum.* Xi'an, China.

— 1997. *The Social Impacts of Tourism.* World Tourism Leaders' Meeting. Manila, Philippines. Madrid.

— 1997. *Tourism: 2020 Vision: Influences, Directional Flows and Key Trends.* Executive Summary. Madrid.

— 1997. *Tourism 2000: Building A Sustainable Future for Asia-Pacific.* Maldives.

— no date. *Framework for the Collection and Publication of Tourism Statistics.* Madrid.